Start to Finish

D0521465

WITHDRAWN

Ironman Edition

Start to Finish

24 WEEKS TO AN ENDURANCE TRIATHLON

IRONMAN TRAINING

by Paul Huddle and Roch Frey
with T. J. Murphy

Meyer & Meyer Sport

IRONMAN® is a registered trademark of World Triathlon Corporation

British Library Cataloguing in Publication Data
A catalogue record for this book is available from the British Library

Start to Finish
Maidenhead: Meyer & Meyer Sport (UK) Ltd., 2004
3rd revised Edition 2013
ISBN 978-1-78255-023-5

© 2004 by Meyer & Meyer Sport (UK) Ltd.
3rd revised Edition 2013
Aachen, Auckland, Beirut, Budapest, Cairo, Cape Town, Dubai, Hägendorf,
Indianapolis, Maidenhead, Singapore, Sydney, Tehran, Wien
Member of the World
Sport Publishers' Association (WSPA)
www.w-s-p-a.org
Printed and bound by: B.O.S.S
ISBN 978-1-78255-023-5
E-Mail: info@m-m-sports.com
www.m-m-sports.com

Contents

ACKNOWLEDGEMENTS

The experience and knowledge that we've been able to accumulate and put forward in this book is the result of the contributions of many people. This list includes but is not limited to fellow athletes, coaches, friends, family members, race organizers, athletes we've coached, and the people responsible for having the patience to deal with us in compiling this information.

We feel fortunate to have been at "the right place at the right time" in terms of the generation of athletes we trained, raced, and lived with over the years. If learning is experiential, these were our fellow students and teachers: Kenny Langone, John Clothier, Jimmy Riccitello, Scott Tinley, Mark Allen, Michellie Jones, Mike Pigg, Ray Browning, Greg Welch, Kenny Souza, Mark Montgomery, and too many others to list here.

Every athlete has had a coach. While our sport was too young to have coaches who were focused on triathlon as a sport in and of itself, we had single sport coaches who helped us form our training philosophy and methods. Those include, but are not limited to: Mark Yellin, Paul Williams, Dave Murray, Jane Scott, Ron Marcicick, and John Howard. Those who helped confirm triathlon coaching concepts through clinics and their writing include Joe Friel, Gale Bernhardt, Rick Nyles, Dr. Edmund Burke, Dr. John Hogg, Dave Johnson, and Dr. Tim Noakes.

The biggest influences on our lives, and hence, this book have been our families and spouses. Paula Newby-Fraser and Heather Fuhr are not just world champion triathletes but best friends, confidantes and partners in life.

Finally, writing a book is a process for which we were decidedly unprepared. While we had the material in hand, getting these words on paper in an organized and useful format was the result of a lot of hard work by three people — Bob Babbitt, T.J. Murphy and Beth Hagman. To say that this book would not have been possible without the efforts of these three is not just an understatement but a glaring fact. We are indebted to each of you.

FOREWORD

I first worked with Paul Huddle and Roch Frey when I was editor of Triathlete Magazine. They proposed taking on a monthly question-and-answer column, and we leaped at the idea.

The two coaches were working with some of the best pros in the sport and they'd long been high-caliber triathletes themselves. In addition to the pros they coached, they'd worked with legions of age-groupers from the virgin beginner to blazing hotshot. In other words, they knew our readership's wants and needs, obstacles and frustrations.

It didn't take long for "Dear Coach" to become one of the most popular pages in the magazine.

My personal feeling as to why is revealed in the story of the photos they sent to go along with their first columns: an envelope containing color snapshots of themselves posing with surfboards. In the often stiff and unrelenting territory of endurance training editorial, Roch Frey and Paul Huddle, in both prose and portrait, had an original and entertaining voice.

Infusing a sense of humor into their coaching is more than a teaching aid. Their athletes, particularly the ones training for Ironman-distance events, become all the more grounded. The pressure and fear and uncertainty of preparing for such a complex and demanding feat is taxing in itself, and Huddle and Frey's guidance is accompanied by a relief valve.

The result? Triathletes not only blow the roof off their fitness level, but find time to smile while doing it. The humorous slant (to which Huddle credits intensive study of Fast Times at Ridgemont High) keeps athletes relaxed and free from being completely overwrought.

Another feature they bring to their coaching is a balanced mix of hard science and not-so-scientific secrets plucked from the boundaries pushed by the elite.

As the highly-regarded sports scientist Dr. Randy Eichner of the University of Oklahoma has said, world class athletes work and gain information from a frontier not immediately accessible to the number-crunching techniques of scientific method.

Huddle and Frey honor both realms. They study the science of sport like mad, comparing findings with their many levels of triathlon field work. When Heather Fuhr, Paula Newby-Fraser and Peter Reid discover something with potential, it is digested by the coaches and relayed to those further back in the pack. Beneficiaries include triathletes making their first run at the Ironman distance as well as the more seasoned age-grouper trying to strip another hour off their PR. No one has all the answers, but Huddle and Frey have a lot of them. In following the program included in this book, you can confidently focus your energy on training instead of leaking it away on worrying if what you're doing is "right." This equation doesn't accurately translate into "fun," however — as the great American distance running coach, Joe Vigil, warns: "Satisfaction," says Vigil, "is what you get out of working hard toward a hard goal."

Follow the program in this book with vigilance and passion, and satisfaction will be yours to claim.

T. J. Murphy

INTRODUCTION

Put the book down. Put the book down and slowly back away from your first step into what could end up being a lifelong love (addiction) with (to) Ironman (the hard stuff). Maybe you started with a single sport (beer) like swimming, cycling, or running. Bored with the monotony of one discipline, you sampled and fell in love with the sport of triathlon (pot). Now, you've either seen it on TV and thought, "Wow, I'd love to do that!" or you're simply tired of being asked, "Oh, you do triathlon? Have you done that race in Hawaii?" and now want to take the next logical step up to the Ironman distance (the hard stuff). We understand.

© Paul Huddle by Lois Schwartz

We understand and we want to help you achieve your goal in the best way possible while limiting your risk of losing your job, friends, and family along the way.

All joking aside, training for and executing an Ironman triathlon is, for most people, the endurance sport challenge of a lifetime. The very notion of swimming 2.4 miles in open water, cycling 112 miles, and running a full 26.2-mile marathon in less than 17 hours, while exposed to whatever conditions Mother Nature has in store, is intimidating — to say the least. What would possess any sane person to take on such a challenge in an age of comfort and convenience?

The answers are as varied as the participants, but all seem to have a common thread that is joined at the root by our most primal modes of self-propelled human transportation through varied earthly environments (swimming, cycling, and running) and some seemingly genetically encoded need to move.

What will this book give you that you couldn't get in another? We've been able to distill a wide variety of information and experience from the sport of triathlon as a whole down to the specifics that pertain to preparing for and completing an Ironman distance event. That was the goal. While there are necessarily some related topics, all of them are aimed at the Ironman distance. We wanted to create a resource that was specific and simple. Training for an event of this distance with three different disciplines invites complication, but there is also a simplicity that can be found common to all endurance training.

I recall a lengthy conversation on a run with a top professional in which we discussed all of the intricate details of a final build-up in preparation for an Ironman. By the end of the run, I was chuckling to myself at all of the analysis. He asked what I was laughing at.

I replied, "It's all pretty simple. Swim a lot, ride a lot and run a lot. Rest a lot. Then race."

We stand by that statement. Yes, there are a million ways you can combine each discipline and the intensities and duration of workouts but, in its essence, it boils down to specificity of training, which, in the case of an Ironman, involves a lot of swimming, cycling and running followed by recovery and the event.

The early chapters will give you the basics that we feel every Ironman athlete needs in order to embark on their journey to the finish line. We will discuss the basic principles underlying our approach to triathlon and Ironman training. This includes the fundamentals Ironman training requires, as well as the essential vocabulary you'll need before the first workout of the training program itself.

The heart of the book is the actual 24-week training program laid out in Chapters five through eight in six-week increments. This represents the day-by-day, week-by-week work to be done in preparing for a successful ironman.

In Chapters nine through 11, we'll take care of several of the finer points surrounding the Ironman, including tips and strategies for race week, nutrition, and a few answers to the more common questions inspired by the event.

Without a doubt, there will be plenty more questions about subjects like equipment, day-to-day nutrition, recovery and technique. This book has purposefully focused on the training itself, leaving the broader topics for other works, including books, videotapes, camps and magazines. Check our resource pages in the appendix for a good place to quench all thirsts for Ironman knowledge.

In purchasing this book, the one question we figured you've already answered is, "Should I do an Ironman?"

With that answer in mind, it's time to become acquainted with the program, Zen out a bit, and get to work.

Paul Huddle

IRONMAN TRAINING PREREQUISITES

To be blunt, you need a foundation coming in. Before you tackle an Ironman, we suggest a minimum of one year's experience training for and racing triathlons. Should you decide to forego this qualification, you certainly won't be the first. However, in terms of safely handling the volume and intensity required, it's smart to spend at least a year exploring the sport's more receptive race distances.

On the day that you are to hurl yourself into our 24-week training program, plan so that you're comfortable with, or have worked up to, a weekly training volume as described here.

Swimming
At least two swim workouts per week, roughly 60 minutes in length. In both sessions, practice drills and stroke exercises described in the Techniques chapter.

Cycling
Three bike rides a week — one long ride of about three hours, and two shorter rides of 60 minutes each. As you work to reach this point, use one of the shorter rides to work on your technique. At the start of the Ironman training, you need to be bike-fit enough so that cycling along at 90RPM is a no-brainer.

Running
Build up to a long run of 90 minutes, with two additional 45-60 minute runs rounding out the week. At the end of one of the shorter runs, work through the drills and accelerations described in the Techniques chapter.

Special Note on Running: If you're coming from a pure cycling or swimming background, with little or no time in running shoes, the following special considerations apply:

As you've probably heard, there are two types of cyclists: those who have crashed and those who are going to crash. The same applies to running and running injuries. Even though you may have a heart of steel, thanks to thousands of hours in the pool or in the saddle, your body is going to need time to adapt to the jarring nature of running. In other words, be patient. Start with where you're at and add no more than 10% a week to your existing volume. Slowly work your way to the minimums above.

CHAPTER 1
Ironman Fundamentals

A good starting point on the path to an Ironman competition is to become acquainted (or reacquainted) with the core principles of the sport. In the early years of the Hawaii Ironman, no one really had any idea how to train for the thing. While only a privileged and talented few will ever be able to claim a measure of mastery over the event, following these principles will allow you to bypass some common mistakes. It will also introduce you to methods we know will help you get the best out of yourself.

BE HONEST ABOUT WHAT YOU'RE GETTING YOURSELF INTO AND MAKE YOUR WORLD RIGHT FOR IT.

Ironman training requires a lot of time, energy and commitment. Before you toss a check into the mailbox (or hand it over to the appropriate officials after qualifying for Hawaii), make sure all hell isn't going to break loose. Try to choose a race date that doesn't come on the tail end of your job's busiest time of year. Talk to your loved ones and rally for their understanding and support.

USE A HEART RATE MONITOR TO PROPERLY GAUGE YOUR TRAINING INTENSITY.

The heart rate monitor takes a lot of the guesswork out of training. It tells you exactly at what intensity and in what system you're training. However, don't dismiss cognitive intuition when using the heart rate monitor, and always listen to what your body tells you. There may be times when you're fatigued from a previous day's hard session and are unable to crank your heart rate up high enough. Rather than pushing too hard, listen to your body and decrease the intensity or length of the workout.

TREAT TRIATHLON AS A SPORT IN ITSELF — NOT A COLLECTION OF THREE SINGLE SPORTS.

This mantra of triathlon training especially applies to the athlete embarking on the road to an Ironman. Since many triathletes come from single-sport backgrounds, they try to apply the same training principles from their primary discipline to the other two. If you tried to train each discipline like a single sport athlete for each of the 2.4-mile swim/112-mile bike/26.2-mile run requirements of an Ironman, you'd take on a schedule that would nosedive into over-training, injury, illness, joblessness and divorce.

In our program, we'll be doing only one high-intensity or key workout in each discipline each week. The core of the program incorporates five "key" workouts each week: one harder (higher intensity) swim, bike and run workout and one longer ride and run. Everything else should be added and adjusted to your strengths and weaknesses, goals and time restraints.

WHEN IT'S CONVENIENT, DON'T HESITATE TO DO BACK-TO-BACK WORKOUTS.

Too many triathletes try to avoid riding after swimming or running after riding. Since the nature of our sport includes swimming, cycling and running in succession, doing this in training helps you prepare for these transitions – and it saves on showers! If you're going to run on the same day that you ride, do your run after riding. This tends to be the most difficult of the two transitions. By doing it frequently in training, it will become much easier when you race. The only exception to this is when you are planning to do a hard or long run. These key workouts need to get priority and should be done first.

NEVER DO A LONG AND/OR HARD BIKE WORKOUT ON THE SAME DAY YOU DO A LONG AND/OR HARD RUN.

For example, do not do your long run on the same day as your high intensity or long bike ride. Since both cycling and running are lower body activities, you'll fatigue these muscles with the first workout and won't be able to get the most out of the second workout. It is okay to do a long or hard swim workout on the same day as a long or hard ride or run, however. Since the primary muscle groups involved in swimming are upper body activities, you won't negatively impact your ability to execute a quality ride or run (or vice versa).

PLAN RECOVERY INTO YOUR TRAINING SCHEDULE.

Once you get rolling in the program, it can become hard to slow down — but all your time and hard work will be of little value without the recovery necessary to absorb it. Juggling work and other commitments with an Ironman training program, you may be tempted to cut hours of sleep and other down-time. Don't do it! Your chances of over-training and the problems associated with it will increase exponentially.

GAINS IN ATHLETIC PERFORMANCE COME FROM CONSISTENT TRAINING OVER A LONG PERIOD OF TIME.

Too many athletes train great for one or two months only to get sick or injured and are then forced to take that time off to recover. It's not how much you did last week that counts, but how consistently you have been training over the past few months. Build toward your Ironman a small, focused piece at a time,

24 weeks of solid preparation come down to this: the start of an Ironman Triathlon.

digesting the work you do, and keeping at it day by day. Trying to do too much too soon will only get you in trouble, as will getting into the habit of skipping workouts. Discipline yourself to be steady, consistent and patient.

DEVELOP YOUR TECHNIQUE IN ALL THREE DISCIPLINES.

Drills are a weekly fixture of our Ironman training program. At first glance, they might seem like only an enhancement to the primary training and are therefore dispensable.

In truth, development of proper form, body position and refined technique is the smartest way to improve your speed in long distance triathlons. Improved technique equates to greater efficiency in each stroke or stride that you take, meaning more ground covered using less energy.

When you're talking about 140.6 miles of composite ground, an inch here and a calorie less there adds up to a lot. This strongly applies to swimming, but to cycling and running as well. Improving your form and technique also lessens your susceptibility to injury.

Injuries, unfortunately, do occur.
If you take time off at the first sign of injury, the opportunity for a quick recovery is best. If you're unsure about a persistent injury or pain, seek out a qualified health professional.

SAVE RACING FOR RACE DAY.

Group training is a great thing. It makes the long, hard workouts easier to show up for and get done. However, don't fall into the trap of racing against your workout buddies. Each workout should be focused toward gaining a specific training effect. If you start racing in an interval workout or on a long bike ride, you've let go of the long term goal in exchange for a quick thrill. Train when training, race when racing.

REMEMBER TO ENJOY THE RIDE.

It's an annual epidemic: each year on the day following the Hawaii Ironman, Kona is awash with athletes despairing over their performance, looking like someone killed their dog. A slow split time, or a lost ten minutes due to a blown tire, or failure to do well enough in their age-group to ascend the award's podium — in a daylong event, there are many opportunities for things to go wrong.

We must now address a truth. Rare is the triathlete who has a perfect race day. After winning six Hawaii titles and retiring, Mark Allen remarked, "Every year I went to the starting line feeling I had it figured out. Every year I was wrong." Allen's point was that it's not whether or not you're going to run into trouble during the race. You will. But, while you can't control the conditions of a race, nor your luck with equipment and the like, you can control your mindset. Try to keep it all in perspective: it's a lifestyle as well as a sport.

CHAPTER 2
Testing & Heart Rate

This is a good place to stop and ask yourself if you even care about specific training intensities. The following, for some athletes, takes the fun and spontaneity out of their sport. Still, once you establish a good connection between sensory input (perceived exertion) during exercise and an accurate, objective measurement (heart rate monitor), you get control of your performance destiny. And we're assuming that, if you're reading this, your intent is to improve your performance in endurance sports.

That said, if you just don't want to bother with the complexities of using a heart rate monitor, it's okay. Using "Perceived Exertion" alone is not a bad way to do this program. The greatest risk is that you'll overdo it rather than "underdo" it. Keep this in mind should you choose this path.

The two criteria we'll discuss are: Rate of Perceived Exertion (RPE) and Heart Rate (HR). While the heart rate monitor (HRM) will give you an accurate reading of what your heart is doing (and allow you to correlate HR with a given training level/zone), your perceived exertion allows you to evaluate how difficult a training session is by assigning numbers to your perception of each incremental level of difficulty. Heart rate monitors provide an external, objective measurement which, though an excellent tool, can't account for factors like environmental conditions, muscle fatigue, psychological states, etc. RPE enables you to subjectively measure your level of effort and, when combined with an HRM, provides a more complete picture of your level of effort.

RATINGS OF PERCEIVED EXERTION

The scale shown was developed in the early 1970s by a Swedish scientist named Dr. Gunnar Borg ("Did I need to know that?"). He determined that athletes could, through a numbered scale, predict accurately how hard they were exercising based on how they felt and correlate these numbers, quite accurately, to heart rate. Some experienced athletes have sharpened their awareness to the degree that they can identify their lactate threshold exactly — just by how they feel. Take a look at these and think about your most recent workout. How would you rate this most recent effort? Begin to connect your true "feelings" of intensity with prescribed levels. Do you feel that a workout isn't worthwhile unless you are in the 16 to 17 range of the original scale? Are you happy staying at or below 12 in all your training? The answers to these questions can indicate trends in your racing performance and provide hints for improvement.

Now that we are familiar with these two determinants of intensity (heart rate & perceived effort), we can combine them for the purpose of communicating how hard or easy a particular workout is to be performed (see chart on next page).

DEFINITIONS

Anaerobic Threshold (AT)* Referred to by some physiologists as the point at which enough anaerobic metabolism occurs that more lactic acid is produced than can be rapidly cleared from the body. This occurs from 60 to 95% of VO2 max, depending on your fitness level. Your AT is where breathing becomes labored but maintainable. If you continue to raise the pace, you soon will hit VO2 max — beyond which you will reach failure (puking and bleeding from your lungs). AT is a trainable level.

Also referred to as lactate threshold.

Rating of Perceived Exertion

Rating	Perceived Effort
6	
7	Very, Very Light
8	
9	Very Light
10	
11	Fairly Light
12	
13	Somewhat Hard
14	
15	Hard
16	
17	Very Hard
18	
19	Very, Very Hard
20	

Maximum Heart Rate (MHR) The highest attainable heart rate is a genetically determined value. Although there are formulas to predict it, the best way to determine your MHR is to actually go out and achieve it. For example, go to a track, warm up 15 minutes, run 1 x 400m hard, 1 x 400m harder, and then 1 x 800m building from hard to all out over the final 300m. Take 1 minute recovery after each 400 and remember to cool down at least 10 minutes (jogging or walking) after the 800. MHR is not a trainable level. It is what it is.

VO2 Max This refers the maximum amount of oxygen you can take in and utilize. In short, this level can only be maintained for one or two minutes before you are forced to stop from exhaustion. Max VO2 is a trainable level.

Aerobic (literally "with oxygen") Generally speaking, this could mean being able to sing your alma mater's fight song or hold a conversation or speak in one-word sentences during exercise. As you can see, there is a broad scope of intensities within the definition. In terms of heart rates, aerobic training occurs above 55% of MHR and below AT (got it?).

Resting Heart Rate Resting heart rate is an easy number to determine. The best time to take it is upon waking in the morning. When you wake up, before you get out of bed, slide your middle and forefinger into the groove on your neck (next to your Adam's apple) to feel for your pulse. Grab a watch or look at your clock, relax, and count the number of pulse beats for fifteen seconds. Multiply this number by four — and that is your RHR in beats per minute or BPM. Getting into the habit of checking it regularly will allow you to keep track of your fitness and warn of overtraining and/or impending illness. You will recognize when you aren't fully recovered from a workout the day before or might be getting sick when you see an increase of five or more BPM.

Anaerobic Threshold Heart Rate (ATHR) Your heart rate when exercising at your AT.

TARGET HEART RATE ZONES

Level 1 / Easy Less than 70% MHR or 77% of ATHR. This could also be called "active rest." This is where you will be in the early season and in between hard workout days during the season. For many people (who, me?), this is the hardest place to be. That feeling of "I'm not working hard enough" seems to be difficult for many people. This is the Zone, however, where you can maintain your fitness while recovering from harder work.

Intensity Determination Table

Rating	Perceived Effort	Prescribed Intensity	% of MHR % of ATHR
6		Level 1	70% MHR
7	Very, Very Light	Easy (active recovery)	77% ATHR
8			
9	Very Light		
10		Level 2	71-80% MHR
11	Fairly Light	Medium (aerobic endurance)	78-90% ATHR
12			
13	Somewhat Hard		
14		Level 3	81-90% MHR
15	Hard	Tempo (steady state)	91-100%ATHR
16			
17	Very Hard	Anaerobic Threshold	
18		Level 4	91%+ MHR
19	Very, Very Hard	Hard (VO2 Max, Hammering!!!)	101%+ ATHR
20			

Level 2 / Medium 71-80% MHR or 78-90% ATHR. This could also be called "aerobic endurance." This is a good Zone to stay in for your long rides and runs, where the focus is on installing the plumbing (circulatory system) and energy systems (mitochondria) into the body that will allow your muscles to work more efficiently. This is a relatively easy Zone to be in, but requires steady, moderate effort.

Level 3 / Tempo 81-90% MHR or 91-100% ATHR. This could also be called "tempo." This is where many people spend most their time, because they "feel like" they're working only when they're at or above 78%. Depending on your level of fitness, the frequency and duration spent in this Zone will either drop you into an over-training abyss or gradually maximize your athletic potential. As you raise your AT, this Zone should feel easier and easier. It is not an "easy" level of intensity, but one that you should be able to hold for long periods. In the early "base building" part of the season, this will be the upper limit of higher intensity training.

Level 4 / Hard 91%+ MHR or 101%+ ATHR. This could be called the "hammer" Zone. You'll be more concerned with this Zone when training for sprint and Olympic-distance triathlons — not Ironman training. Excessive time spent in this Zone will quickly lead to diminishing returns.

TESTING FOR ATHR

One of the most accurate methods for determining max HR and ATHR is to go to an exercise physiologist's lab and get tested in your intended activity. If you don't have access to this, you can perform a fairly accurate test on your own. In the Ironman training program, tests for the run and the bike are scheduled during the third and fourth weeks of your training. These come at a time when you've begun to set the wheels in motion on your training, and a good read on appropriate training intensities is in order.

Before you go out to do this, it is crucial to make sure you are physically ready to attempt such a test (yes, this is the warning/disclaimer). Getting the physical "OK" from your doctor is a prerequisite. Even if you are well trained, this is a good step to take to avoid any possible injury or complication that is lurking.

Before we get into the actual test, we would like to stress an important point regarding HR parameters. Your resting heart rate, max HR, anaerobic threshold HR, VO2 max HR, and target training HR, are all personal numbers. These are unique to you and, therefore, not comparable to others from a competitive point of view.

One other point to keep in mind: You will have differing heart rate parameters in each of the different sports. Generally you can expect your swimming HR to be lower than cycling, and your cycling HR to be lower than that of running.

This is because in running you are supporting your full body weight and using the larger muscle groups of the legs. Cycling, while using these large muscle groups, is a weight-supported activity, which results in a lower HR (unless you are standing up out of the saddle). Swimming uses smaller muscle groups as the prime movers (the arms), while water supports and cools the body.

The recommended test for the bike is taken from Joe Friel's The Cyclist's Training Bible. There are testing protocols for both magnetic trainer and Computrainer users (if you are using a Computrainer, refer to the workout manual). Is this the only way to determine ATHR? No. There are many protocols for testing anaerobic threshold, but this is one that we use and works quite well.

MAGNETIC TRAINER SET-UP

- Test must be done with a stationary bike that accurately displays speed (or watts). You can use your own bike on a stationary trainer with a rear wheel computer hook-up.

- Select "manual" mode.

- You will need an assistant to record information.

- Warm up equipment for 5-10 minutes.

THE TEST

- Throughout the test, you will hold a predetermined speed or power level. Start at 15 mph (or 100 watts) and increase by 1 mph (or 20 watts) every 1.5 minutes until you can no longer continue. Stay seated throughout the test. Shift gears at any time.

- At the end of each 1.5 minutes, tell your assistant how great your exertion is, using the original Borg scale (place it where it can be seen).

- Your assistant will record your exertion rating and your heart rate at the end of each 1.5 minutes and instruct you to increase speed (watts) to the next level.

- The assistant will also listen closely to your breathing to detect when it becomes unnaturally labored. This point is the "VT" or ventilatory threshold.

- Continue until you can no longer hold the speed (watts) for at least 15 seconds.

- The data collected should look something like this:

Speed	Power	Heart Rate	Exertion
15	100	110	9
16	120	118	11
17	140	125	12
18	160	135	13
19	180	142	14
20	200	147	15
21	220	153	17 "VT"
22	240	156	19
23	260	159	20

- Compare "VT" heart rate/power with an exertion rating in the range of 16-18 to determine lactate threshold (anaerobic threshold). To help confirm this, realize that athletes are seldom able to go more than five minutes beyond their lactate threshold (anaerobic thresholds) on this test. You now have an estimate of anaerobic threshold to compare with other indicators, including actual race (time-trial) heart rates and subsequent tests.

RUNNING ATHR TEST

Executed in a similar fashion to the bike test, but on a treadmill, (increasing speed in .1 or .2 mph increments).

OR: Schedule a 10K road race on the fifth weekend of your Ironman training, which would replace your long run for the week. Wear a heart rate monitor and record an average heart rate for the event. The average will be your ATHR for running.

ON THE SWIM

It's difficult to accurately test for heart rates in the water and to use Zones while training for swimming. For this reason, we suggest that you use perceived effort in the pool. Finding your heart rate between sets can help determine training adaptation and conditioning. Simply take your heart rate with your index and third finger at your neck (carotid artery) after completion of a hard main set and then take your heart rate again 1 minute later. Take note of the difference between the two heart rates. As your fitness increases, you will recover faster and see this number increase.

Train with a partner! The benefits include safety, camaraderie, support, motivation and challenge. If you don't have one already, find a partner or workout group through your local tri club, better bike shops, or by asking around at events.

SETTING UP TARGET HEART RATES

Now that you know your anaerobic threshold HR, you can use it to gauge the intensity of your workouts depending on the time of the season you're in and on your race-specific goals. These levels of intensity can be broken up into 3 to 5 HR ranges or Zones. Throughout the training week, your day-to-day target HR will change according to the workout given, as well as the purpose of that workout. During the adaptation and base phases, the majority of your training hours should be spent below ATHR.

Calculate your different target Zones based on your ATHR heart rate* in the different sports.

Example: My anaerobic threshold heart rate (ATHR) for running is tested to be 170 beats per minute. Since the "easy" or "active rest" Zone is 77% ATHR, my easy Zone for running is:

.77 X 170 = 130.9 or 131

In other words, my easy Zone is less than 131 bpm.

Target Zone Worksheet

	Swimming	Cycling	Running
HR#1 ‹70% MHR or ‹77% of ATHR			
HR#2 71-80% MHR or 78-90% ATHR			
HR#3 81-90% MHR or 91-100% ATHR			
HR#4 91%+ MHR or 101%+ ATHR			

*If using your MHR, simply insert the corresponding % into each training intensity level

AT Heart Rate Evaluation Form

Name

Resting HR   Cal.#   Date

Time (minutes)	Workload (watts/speed)	Heart Rate (bpm)	Perceived Exertion 7 (easiest) to 20 (hardest)
0:00 to 5 - 10:00	Warm Up		
0:00 - 1:30	100 watts		
1:30 - 3:00	120		
3:00 - 4:30	‹140		
4:30 - 6:00	160		
6:00 - 7:30	180		
7:30 - 9:00	200		
9:00 - 10:30	220		
10:30 - 12:00	240		
12:00 - 13:30	260		
13:30 - 15:00	280		
15:00 - 16:30	300		
16:30 - 18:00	320		
18:00 - 19:30	340		
19:30 - 21:00	360		
21:00 - 22:30	380		
22:30 - 24:00	400		
24:00 - 25:30	420		
25:30 - 27:00	440		
27:00 - 28:30	460		
28:30 - 30:00	480		
30:00 - 31:30	500		
31:30 - 33:00	520		
33:00 - 34:30	540		

At the end of the day, you'll appreciate the real value of pacing.

CHAPTER 3
Terminology & Techniques

Our 24-week Ironman training program is organized into four six-week phases. Assuming you're coming off a break or you're at the season's start, we begin with an adaptation phase that reacquaints your mind and body to the rhythm of training. We steadily build from there toward a peak of hard, Ironman-specific training weeks. After that, you'll taper for three weeks in the lead-up to the race. Executed with desire and discipline, the six-month plan will prepare you to perform well in a 2.4-mile swim/112-mile bike/26.2-mile run competition.

In this chapter, we will brief you on the techniques and vocabulary we put to use in the program. First, let's break down the phases.

WEEKS 1-6: ADAPTATION PHASE

Purpose: Getting into the groove of training, waking up your technique and installing the aerobic "plumbing" necessary for the training stress to come.

WEEKS 7-12: AEROBIC BASE

Purpose: Focusing on strength and taking another step toward being able to handle Ironman-specific training.

WEEKS 13-18: IRONMAN-SPECIFIC BASE

Purpose: The first three weeks of this phase will finish preparing you for a hard, Ironman training program, which will immediately begin upon the start of the second three-week period of this phase.

WEEKS 19-24: RACE PHASE

The first half of this phase will include more hard Ironman-specific training. The final three-week countdown to your race will be a smart, gradual taper that will let your body digest all the hard work you've done and sharpen you up for a best effort.

ALTERNATIVES

THE 9-WEEK IRONMAN TRAINING PROGRAM

If you're already strong and fit from your standard triathlon training and racing regimen, you can skip to the 16th week in the program, and start from there.

THE "BARE MINIMUM"

As you'll see when you read through the training schedules, the program demands at least one thing of you: time. If work and other priorities have a certain inflexibility and your primary goal is simply to snag a finisher's medal and T-shirt, no problem. You can follow a pared-down program by completing only the "key" workouts within each week, and skip the rest.

MASTERS SWIMMING

Is it okay to substitute Masters swimming with the prescribed swim workouts? Yes. In fact, there's no better way to improve your stroke and swimming capability than working consistently with a good coach in a good program. To find a Masters program near you, visit the governing body's website: www.usms.org.

TRAINING TECHNIQUES

The specific workouts in this program are based on duration and intensity. The three types of workouts include the following:

1. EASY RECOVERY DAYS

As the name implies, the purpose of these workouts is to recover and absorb the harder training while honing and maintaining technique. These workouts are generally performed at HR#1-2.

2. HIGHER INTENSITY DAYS

These are your high-quality "key" workouts. The intensity will depend on the phase you're training in. All quality sessions include a warm-up, a main set and a cool-down. HR#2-4.

3. LONGER AEROBIC DAYS

While the intensity of these sessions could be confused with easy recovery days, the duration is significantly longer. The purpose of this session is geared to the development of the aerobic and fat metabolizing systems. Basically, you are trying to establish the plumbing (capillaries/ mitochondria) and specific joint/muscle strength that will enable you to handle the stresses of the pre-competitive and competitive phases.

DRILLS AND WORKOUTS

It's now time to talk about the drills and workouts specific to each discipline. Since we're assuming you have a solid triathlon background, most of this should be review.

SWIMMING

Swimming is the most challenging discipline of the three in the area of technique. As we mentioned earlier, the best favor you can do yourself before launching into this program is to learn how to swim correctly. Swimming classes, triathlon camps, seminars like Terry Laughlin's "Fish-like Swimming" workshops, and Masters swimming programs are almost necessities for those coming into Ironman training without a good swimming background. Videos are another option. Check the Resources chapter for information.

The race clock is not the only thing to be concerned with when finishing the swim at an Ironman. For most of us, performing well in the swim means getting out of the water having used as little energy as possible. With lots of hard biking and running on the to-do list, every calorie spared is precious. Greater efficiency is your goal when it comes to swim training.

When in doubt, favor technique over speed. Throughout the 24-week program, we'll ask you to continue to drill yourself on the basics and to continue to monitor your form. Here's a description of the basics:

SWIM DRILLS

1. Kick with your arms at your side. Focus on keeping the body in one plane of water... press the chest forward to help keep the hips up, keep the head down (do not bury the chin, however). When you need a breath, roll to one side or the other, take the breath, and then roll slowly and smoothly back to your stomach. For most people, this is the hardest of the freestyle drills to master.

2. Kick on your side. Keeping your chin, cheek or ear into your shoulder and your right arm outstretched in front of you, kick on your right side. The left arm rests on your side, with your left hand on your hip; your left arm will break the surface of the water. Follow the same pattern on the left side of your body.

3. Kick from side to side (S2S). Starting on one side, do a series of 6-9 kicks with your legs, then recover the arm resting on your side to the top of your stroke and meet the other hand (known as catch up) and pull through to the other side.

It's important to maintain horizontal body positioning in the water while rolling from one side to the other. Breathe to the left as you pull your left arm, and

SWIM TECHNIQUE CHECKLIST

Head   Looking down and slightly forward. Water level between center of head and forehead.

Hips   Up close to the surface and rolling completely from side to side during each arm stroke.

Feet   Up close to the surface with heels slightly breaking the surface while kicking.

Kicking   Gentle kick of one to two feet in width.
Kick should start from the hips with slight bending of the knees and ankles. Toes pointed and relaxed.

Body Length   Long straight body all moving as one unit.
No bending at the waist or independent twisting of the upper and lower body.

Body Roll   Roll from side to side as one unit. Hips and shoulders should start to roll at the start of the pull and roll completely to the side by the end of the pull.

Lay-out Free   Best Drill for practicing body roll and getting used to swimming on your side. Four seconds on each side while fully catching-up between strokes.

Catch-up Free   Continuous free with catching up of the arms in front before pulling. Do not pause at the finish of the stroke. Three second catch with proper roll.

Cheating Catch-Up Free   The fastest and most efficient freestyle stroke.
Smooth exchange of the arms in front with an almost catch-up.
Full body roll and long body position.

to the right as you pull your right arm. If you need additional breaths before rotating from one side to another, that is fine. Just try not to breathe as you recover one of your arms.

4. Catch-up (C/U). Without any pause at the back end of the stroke, pull one arm through a complete stroke cycle and have one hand meet the other prior to starting the next stroke cycle.

5. Cheating Catch-up, also called FREESTYLE or SWIM – The actual swimming style we want to see... the end result. Just as the left hand passes the head, start moving the right side of your hip to the other side, and begin pulling with the right arm. The left arm should enter the water before the right arm is more than one-third of the way through its pull.

Focused drills need to be part of every swim workout, because it's more important to swim efficiently than to swim fast. Every bit of the energy you save in those first 2.4 miles will be needed later. Masters Swimming programs and workshops like Total Immersion will help a lot.

CYCLING

The bike training in the program is divided between easy rides, long aerobic rides, and high-intensity sessions on a turbo-trainer.

Turbo: When we say turbo-trainer, by the way, we're referring to an indoor cycling resistance machine attached to your bike. Computrainers are our favorites, but there are many others available. A bike computer and heart rate monitor, teamed with a magnetic resistance trainer, can turn your bike into an amateur exercise physiology lab. Turbo trainer workouts develop power, a good pedal stroke and speed endurance. If you don't already have the equipment you need for a turbo workout, now's the time to acquire it, even if you have to beg, borrow or steal.

INTENSITY WORKOUT TERMINOLOGY

Most of the bike workouts in the program are self-explanatory, but the turbo sessions are a bit cryptic. Here's a primer.

Sample workout:
* 15 minutes warm-up
* 4 x 40 seconds SLD (Single Leg Drills), 20 seconds recovery both legs
* 3 x 5 minute Big Gear Intervals at HR#2 as:
    2 minutes in big gear < 80 RPM
    1 minute in smaller gear >100RPM
    2 minutes back in big gear < 80 RPM
    2 minutes recovery
* 4 x 30 seconds fast spin, 30 seconds recovery
* 10 minutes cool-down

In English:
After warming up for at least 15 minutes, roll right into the single leg drills. "4 x 40 seconds, 20 seconds recovery both legs," means you will spin with one leg for 40 seconds, 20 seconds with both legs, then 40 seconds with the other leg followed by 20 seconds with both legs again. This is one repetition (1 x 40 seconds on each leg).

"3 x 5 min Big Gear Intervals at HR#2 as 2 minutes in big gear < 80 RPM/ 1 min in smaller gear > 100RPM/ 2 minutes back in big gear < 80 RPM, 2 min recovery" entails 3 sets of 5 minutes as follows: the first two minutes are in a bigger gear

CYCLING: THE IRONMAN POSITION

The biggest difference between effective road and aero positions is the point of contact between the cyclist and bicycle. A road rider contacts the bike with his feet, butt and hands, while a triathlete (aero position) contacts the bike with his feet, butt, and elbows. In order for a triathlete to maintain comfort and performance in an aero position, changes away from a typical road position need to be made.

When you've established an aero position, following the checklist provided on the next page, it's important to dial it back a notch or two for comfort rather than pure aero-dynamics. You're going to be on the bike a long time, and if you can't stay in the aero position because your back hurts, aerobars become worthless. Use your long rides to experiment and confirm the position early in your training.

(higher resistance) at a slower leg turnover (less than 80 RPM) followed by 1 min in smaller gear (lower resistance) at a faster leg turnover (greater than 100 RPM), and then back into a bigger gear (the same as the first two minutes). Throughout the entire five-minute effort, your heart rate should stay in Zone 2. After each 5 min effort, you have a two-minute recovery in which you should keep pedaling at a cadence of 80-100 RPM but with a low enough resistance to allow your heart rate to recover down into Zone 1.

"4 x 30 seconds fast spin, 30 seconds recovery" means 30 seconds of fast spinning in a smaller gear with low resistance while keeping the RPMs as high as possible and maintaining smooth pedaling (no bouncing butts). The 30 seconds recovery is back down into a normal RPM of 80-100. Finish the session with 10-15 minutes of easy spinning at your own pace.

TURBO DRILL DESCRIPTIONS

SLD - Single Leg Drills These drills are exactly what they sound like. The goal of this drill is to make your pedal stroke more efficient. In order to do this, we need to isolate each leg while remaining in a normal riding position (no leaning sideways or funky postures!). Try to make sure that the foot rest is at least bottom bracket high and out of the crank/pedal rotational path (options include: used milk crates, wastebaskets turned upside down, tied stacks of newspaper, or simply rest your foot behind you on your trainer's mounting brackets — without catching your feet in the spokes or fan blades) on either side of your bicycle.

When working one leg, try to be smooth, feel the entire circle of the pedal stroke, and keep your RPMs above 80-90. Maintain the position you race in and note the difference in power when sitting up (torso-femur angle open) compared to your aero position (torso-femur angle more closed). This may indicate what might be a faster, more powerful and more comfortable (but, perhaps, not as "aero") position.

Initially, it is likely you will use your smallest (easiest) gear for single leg drills but, as you practice this drill over time consistently, you will improve to the point of using bigger gears and/or sustaining the drill for a longer period of time. The main point to remember is to be as smooth as possible (try to get your turbo trainer to hum rather than making a voom-voom-voom sound). Pedal in circles, not squares.

Big Gear Intervals As the name implies, these intervals are performed in a big gear at lower RPMs than normal. This is like strength training on the bike. It teaches you to push a bigger gear efficiently, developing strength that will help you with time trialing and seated climbing. Stay seated and work the entire circle of the pedal stroke. Many cyclists feel they can generate more power when sliding slightly toward the rear of the saddle. Experiment with different positions. Most big gear intervals are performed in high Zone 2 to low Zone 3 (these are not anaerobic threshold workouts).

Fast Spinning Drills Spinning at higher than normal RPM intervals teaches your cycling muscles to fire at a higher than normal rate. This will translate into greater economy at your normal cadence and make harder or faster riding less stressful. After performing spinning drills at 120+ RPMs, a cadence of 90-100 feels effortless and makes you efficient at a wider range of pedaling cadences. Spinning drills should be performed in your smaller gears with little resistance.

BIKE: AERO POSITION CHECKLIST

Saddle   The tip of the saddle ranges from an inch behind to a half-inch in front of the center of the bottom bracket. The saddle tilt should be such that the front two to three inches (the narrow part) is parallel to the top tube. Because of the shape of some saddles, the rear will be higher than the front giving the illusion of a downward tilt.

Leg Length   Optimal leg length is achieved when the angle between the femur and the lower leg is between 145-150 degrees (some people measure the opposite angles of 30-35 degrees). If you can't measure the angle, dangle your unclipped foot with your arch over the pedal. With cycling shoes on, your arch should just touch the pedal. Barefoot, your arch should be 1/8 to 1/4 of an inch (1/2 centimeter) above the pedal surface. When measuring in this manner, make sure your hips are not tilted to one side or the other.

Aerobars   An optimal aero position puts your shoulders directly above or slightly behind your elbows when resting on the pads. If you are still too stretched out, make adjustments by shortening the stem and/or changing the length of the aero bars (most aero bars come in different lengths or are adjustable). It is best to use aero bars that allow the pads to be slightly behind the center of the bars (i.e.: Syntace). In the aero position, the pads should be slightly in front of your elbows and shoulder-width apart. The angle of the aero bars (tilting up or down) can be based on personal preference. Many athletes like their bars to be parallel to the ground or slightly angled up. Try several different positions to determine which feels best for you.

Maintaining even pressure on the pedal at higher RPMs and low resistance develops fine neuromuscular motor control. Follow each effort with easy spinning at a comfortable cadence.

Since the goal of these drills is efficiency and economy, you don't need to worry about your heart rate. It may go up briefly but, due to the short duration, the effort will be alactate (very little lactic acid will be produced).

RUNNING

Running workouts during a "typical" training week can be defined as intensity (intervals/track or fartlek), long, or recovery runs. All of these runs include a warm-up into the main portion of the run, followed by a cool-down.

TRACK WORKOUTS/FARTLEK RUNNING

Higher intensity runs can be performed as either track workouts or *fartlek* (Swedish for *speed play*) runs. Fartlek running can be as structured or unstructured as the individual would like. A structured fartlek run might be done on a favorite loop and would include a warm-up followed by a main set and cool down.

Structured example: 10-15 minute warm up, 5 x 2 min at HR#3, 1 minute recovery at HR#1-2, 10-15 minute cool down.

An unstructured fartlek run might include the same warm-up and cool down with an assortment of pick-ups within the middle 15 minutes. You could pick objects in the distance (light poles, telephone poles, parked cars, trees, small dogs), hills, flats or downhills as the distances to "pick it up."

A TYPICAL TRACK WORKOUT

Warm up (two to three miles or 15 minutes minimum) on the road ending at the track. Take a final potty stop and put on your racing flats (if you wear racing shoes in races, this is a good opportunity to get adjusted to them). This shouldn't take more than a couple of minutes. Run these two to three laps clockwise (against the correct counterclockwise direction that running on the track is done), gradually accelerate down the straights and then slow to a jog on the turns. The purpose of these is to get your body up to the pace you want to run your intervals with a minimum of shock to your system. After the last acceleration, turn around (yes, DO run in the standard direction) and jog the 100 meters to the start of whatever workout is planned for the day.

A common session would be 8 x 400m with 200m recovery jog in between. As the season progresses, you should be able to increase the pace of the recovery without slowing the pace of the 400s. After the last 400, you can walk 100m or so and then jog a lap, put on your training shoes (if you switched shoes for the workout) and cool down for another 2 to 3 miles (minimum 15 minutes).

STRIDES/ACCELERATIONS AND FORM DRILLS

Many runners complain of lack of leg speed and poor efficiency in their running mechanics. Although your bio-mechanics are inherited to a certain extent, there are some things that can be done to improve both speed and efficiency. Strides and accelerations:

- only take 15-20 minutes once or twice a week
- aren't "painful" (in the anaerobic sense of the word);
- and, combined with consistent moderate running (no intervals), will make you a faster runner.

For this reason, you'll find strides and accelerations written into the schedule with an option of Thursdays or Fridays. We also suggest adding in another at the end of your Tuesday or Saturday transition runs.

Find a 10 to 140 meter stretch of nice grass (a football field at the local high-school is great). If this stretch is on a gradual slope, so much the better. The "workout" goes as follows:

- 2 x 40-80 steps of high knees
- 2 x 40-80 steps of butt kicks
- 2 x 25-50 steps of skipping
- 4-10 x 100-120 meter strides/accelerations (the first 2-5 for form and the second 2-5 for leg speed)

All of the drills should be performed on your toes/forefoot (it will happen naturally) and at a high rate (quick feet!).

What is described on the following pages isn't anything new, but, done consistently, can make improvements in both leg speed and running economy ...and that, after all, is what you're after.

High Knees This drill is done just how it sounds. Maintaining a normal running posture, you exaggerate the knee lift portion of your stride. Arm action is also slightly exaggerated. The knee comes up to, but not beyond, the height of the hip.

Butt Kicks This drill emphasizes the recovery or heel-to-butt portion of the stride. There is no knee lift in this drill but, as the heel comes up to your rear, the knee will naturally move forward. You are simply maintaining normal posture and slightly exaggerated arm action while flicking your heels up to your butt. The biggest mistake you can make is in leaning forward too far. Strive to maintain normal posture and keep your feet underneath your hips.

Skipping Do you know how to skip? This is the same thing, but you are driving your knee up and extending the rear leg in an exaggerated full stride. Skip on the extended leg and do the same thing on the other side, continuing down the field in front of God and everybody. Arms are slightly exaggerated and must be synchronized properly (right arm/left leg, left leg/right arm).

COMMON MISTAKES INCLUDE:

- Incorrect synchronization of arms and legs. Remember that when your left knee is up, your right arm is forward and up.

- Too much bouncing up and down. Think about limiting the amount of time each foot spends on the ground while keeping your body (hips up to head) in one plane.

- An overly upright-leaning back posture (knees coming up higher than the hips). Posture should remain as though you were running (straight up to slight forward lean, depending on who you are, with eyes looking about 10-15 meters ahead) normally.

Note: The purpose of these drills is to exaggerate the different stages of a running stride. You are not interested in getting down the field at a fast pace but focused on proper execution of the drill.

STRIDES/ACCELERATIONS

You could also call these sprints... but they're not. When you think of sprinting, it usually involves out-of-control flailing to escape a pursuing carnivore. Strides are more along the lines of trying to emulate an image of perfect running form: Carl Lewis floating through a 200 meter final or Michael Johnson cruising the back straight during the 400. The first half of the strides are for form. Having an image in your head (such as above), do 2-5 x 100 meters mimicking that image. You are going faster than any race pace but are totally in control. The second half of the strides are to develop leg speed. Concentrate on moving your arms (and legs) as fast as they will possibly go (think "quick feet"). Again, in the back of your head, you are thinking control and form, but the focus here is to fire those running-specific motor neurons as fast as possible.

At the end of each stride, walk, stretch, and "shake it out" until you are ready for the next one. This is not something that should be difficult anaerobically. You may feel briefly winded but should allow complete recovery before beginning the next effort.

RUNNING DRILLS:

TECHNIQUE CHECKLIST

Synchronize — Remember that when your left knee is up, your right arm is forward and up (just like when you run). Don't forget your arms.

Limit Bounce — Make an effort to limit bouncing up and down when doing your drills. It is possible to limit vertical oscillation (bouncing) by focusing on lifting the foot off the ground (not placing the foot on the ground). Think about limiting the amount of time the foot spends on the ground while keeping your body (hips up to head) in one plane.

Lean Into It — An overly upright-leaning back posture (knees coming up higher than the hips) is one of the most common mistakes in performing drills. Posture should remain as though you were running (straight up to slight forward lean, depending on who you are, with eyes looking about 10-15 meters ahead) normally.

Be Consistent — Don't underestimate the value of these drills and the more efficient running technique they cultivate. In a long race like an Ironman, moving faster with a minimum expenditure of energy is paramount. Do these drills at least once a week; you'll reap the rewards.

QUESTIONS & ANSWERS

Q. How should I adjust my bike position for an Ironman?

A. While you can handle an aggressive aero position in an Olympic distance event, you have to dial it back for an Ironman. Aero-bars are worthless if you have to prop yourself up all the time to relieve your back. Your first concern for your race day bike position is comfort. We suggest having an expert at a bike shop or triathlon camp help you. Once you find a zone for comfort, you can tweak for as much power as possible within that zone.

While we're on the topic, be sure to figure out this position before you get into the final six weeks of training. You can use your turbo workouts to adapt to the position throughout the training program, and at minimum, the last eight weeks of the program.

Q. I have a problem with swimming in open water. Frankly, I get freaked out. I have read a lot of articles about people who have panicked during the swim, but never anything on how to counter this problem. Please give me some good sound advice.

A. Your problem isn't uncommon, but it's not something most triathletes like to admit. Swimming in open water isn't the most comfortable thing in the world, no matter who you are. If you allow your mind to wander back to all of the scary movies (Jaws, etc.) before or during your swim, it can not only distract you from the task at hand (swimming as quickly as possible over the course in front of you), but it can set a bad tone for the rest of your race. Most people are much more comfortable in a group situation, but this doesn't always solve the problem.

Beyond suggesting therapy (for hydrophobia? or open-hydrophobia?), we recommend you practice in open water! Face your fears and, by doing so on a regular basis, you'll become more comfortable. I'd get a willing partner (preferably someone who doesn't share your fear — it's always a good idea to swim with someone else in open water situations) or two and do at least one open water swim a week.

Here in the San Diego area, many local triathletes congregate at La Jolla Cove on Friday evenings. This isn't just because misery loves company. The truth is, most of us are a bit freaked out when swimming alone in a large body of water.

Q. I want to buy a good race bike. Any suggestions? How much is too much to spend?

A. Every bike company makes a great bike. There's nothing better to bring out the 10-year-old in yourself than bike shopping. Huddle remembers getting his hands on one particularly hi-tech, artfully designed time trial bike and was giddy. Yet on the first ride, as in all first rides, the truth dawned: "I still have to pedal it!"

The truth also includes the fact that at the 1988 Ironman Japan, Dave Scott loaded his Centurion into the transition area with nothing more than 32-spoked wheels and figs taped to the handlebars. He rode that bare-bones bike on his way to an 8:01 performance.

That said, our advice is mainly this: Get a bike you like. If you think you'll ride faster on it, you will ride faster on it.

Besides this, we offer a warning: Should you go the route of an extremely exotic bike with exotic parts, it can be hard to find replacement parts in some race locales should something break. Bust a custom-made seat post in Lanzarote, and you're in serious trouble.

A good race bike is generally an excellent investment, but the bottom line is: If you think your bike is faster, you'll probably ride faster.

CHAPTER 4
Weight Training

As you read through the weekly schedules of the training program, you'll notice the weight training assignments. Generally speaking, weight training for the Ironman triathlete is seen as a supplement to the main program. We beg to differ. With a race desperate to exhaust your muscles from nearly every imaginable direction, having logged proper gym rat time is an integral defense.

WHY WEIGHTS?

If you're coming into triathlon from an athletic background that relied on explosive power development, maybe weights aren't the best idea right now. Someone who played linebacker at Nebraska, for example, might be better off avoiding the weight room and focusing on cardiovascular development.

For most everyone else, two smartly scheduled weight training workouts per week, during the first three phases of your buildup, will pay off big in power, injury prevention, and in the fluidity of your race day transitions.

The hardest thing about strength training in the program is the increased level of fatigue and the sluggishness experienced in all three sports during this time. While there will be some extra pounds put on, this additional bulk will come off with the more demanding weeks waiting for you in the two months before the race. The gains in injury prevention and performance far outweigh any early season misgivings.

WEIGHTS FOR IRONMAN TRAINING

WARM UP WELL

Arguably the most important part of any workout is the warm-up. What you do in those first 10-15 minutes can mean the difference between a great session and a few weeks or months on your butt due to injury. Always, always, always, warm up!!!

Exactly what you do isn't as important as making sure your muscles are warm and supple. In addition to warming up generally, the following two exercises will help warm up the old body further. They are called the "total body warm-up" and "robot arms" (prepare for the most boring paragraph of your life).

TOTAL BODY WARM-UP AND ROBOT ARMS

The total body warm-up consists of taking a 10 to 25 pound dumbbell and, with your legs shoulder width plus about 6 inches apart, toes pointing slightly out, holding the dumbbell with both hands, raise the weight from its hanging position below your waist line to above your head until your arms are straight and the dumbbell is directly above your head. Now, keeping your elbows in line with your ears, allow the weight to lower down behind your head exactly like a triceps extension. Pause momentarily and smoothly raise the weight back up and as it goes over your head and then past your waist allow your arms to hang straight with the weight and continue through to a squat (if this is possible for you) not past 90 degrees with your legs. Again, pause, and come back up through the whole motion. Repeat this in a smooth slow manner 10 to 15 times. Robot arms are simply a running motion with your arms holding 2.5 to 10 pound dumbbells in each hand. Although this is a warm-up exercise, it is also a great sport-specific motion. Done properly, the arms are held in a normal running position (elbows at 90 degrees or less) and the legs are set one forward and one behind in an unexaggerated frozen gait. The rate of arm swing should be slightly faster than a 5K race pace turnover. Count 50 cycles (50 swings with each arm) and then switch legs and go another 50.

ORDER OF EXERCISES

The order of exercises should be carried out using the large muscle groups (squats, leg extension and curl, bench press, lat pulldown etc.) first, working toward the smaller muscle groups (biceps, triceps, deltoids, etc.). This enables you to work the big muscles without tiring the smaller secondary stabilizing muscles first.

PROPER TECHNIQUE

How many times do you see people in a gym benching 200lbs and bouncing it off their chests? How about standing biceps curls with a forward bend and subsequent swing back that allows a much more macho load to be handled? Proper technique means performing the exercise smoothly through the full range of motion, counting one-two on the work (weight raised) phase, a momentary

TOTAL BODY WARM-UP

- Take a 10 to 25 pound dumbbell.
- Stand with your legs shoulder width plus about six inches apart, toes pointing slightly out, holding the dumbbell with both hands.(Fig #1)
- Raise the weight from its hanging position below your waistline to above your head until your arms are straight and the dumbbell is directly above you. (Fig #2)
- Keeping your elbows in line with your ears, allow the weight to drop slowly behind your head, exactly as in a triceps extension. (Fig #3)
- Pause momentarily and smoothly raise the weight back up.
- As it goes over your head and then forward past your waist, allow your arms to hang straight with the weight. (Fig #4)
- Continue through to a squat, but not past 90 degrees with your legs.
- Pause, and come back up, repeating the entire motion slowly and smoothly 10 to 12 times.

pause at the top (to stop momentum), counting one-two-three-four on the rest (weight lowering) phase with another momentary pause at the bottom (again, to put the brakes on momentum). Done properly, you will probably have to decrease the amount of weight on the bar due to the slower speed of execution.

You should exhale on the work (weight raised) phase and inhale on the "rest" (weight lowered) phase. Holding your breath is dangerous when lifting weights. Breathe!

The exercises listed are classic weight training exercises that you're likely familiar with. Whether familiar with them or not, we highly recommend working with a qualified personal trainer for a session or two to make sure your techique is sound. Also check the resource chapter of this book for the video program, *Strength Training for Triathletes and All Endurance Athletes*. The video illustrates the exercises and details the concepts underlying this approach to the weight room.

NUMBER OF REPS

Current literature suggests that two to three sets of 15 is plenty (That's right, more is not better!). Generally speaking, heavier weight and fewer reps builds power and size, while lighter weight with higher reps emphasizes endurance with minimal gains in bulk. When in the endurance phase, your last three reps

© Paula Newby-Fraser by Robert Oliver

1   2   3   4

should feel difficult but not impossible (you should feel fatigued but able to do one more). The best way to decide how much weight to use in each exercise is to estimate the load initially and then make necessary adjustments as the phase progresses. Begin with a lower weight than your ego thinks is possible for the number of reps indicated. As you progress through the program, additional load increases can be made (but with care!). You will be given guidelines throughout each phase regarding the level of effort exerted within each phase.

ROBOT ARMS

- Choose 2.5 to 10 pound dumbbells, one for each hand.
- Hold arms in a normal running position, elbows locked at 90 degrees or less.
- Set one leg forward and one behind in an unexaggerated frozen gait. (Fig #1)
- Swing your arms at slightly faster than a 5K race pace turnover for 50 cycles (50 swings with each arm). (Fig #2)
  Remember, the movement is from the shoulders—not the elbows.
- Switch legs and go another 50 cycles.

PERIODIZED PHASES

You'll find the weight training workouts written in to the Ironman training program on Thursdays and Sundays for 20 of the 24 weeks. Along with the rest of your training, everything is designed to pull you, phase by phase, through an optimal path of development. The final four weeks, as you recover and taper for the race, you'll leave the weight room behind.

1. ADAPTATION (WEEKS 1-6)

Purpose: To train the neuro-muscular system, to learn the skills and techniques of resistance training, and to establish a strength and endurance base.

Speed of Execution: All exercises are done slowly through the full range of motion for each muscle group. Two seconds to lift and four seconds to lower the weight.

Resistance: Light range—starting at one set of 10 repetitions (reps) and working towards three sets of 15 reps (3 x 15) with light to medium weight. Always think progression... add more weight when the resistance seems easier (caution— never sacrifice proper execution for more weight).

2. ENDURANCE (WEEKS 7-12)

Purpose: To increase strength levels and muscular endurance.

Speed of Execution: Slow and controlled.

Resistance: Medium range—2-3 sets of 15 repetitions.

3. POWER (WEEKS 13-16)

Purpose: To increase strength and power prior to the season while maintaining endurance. You'll note, in this phase of the program, we give the option of "power or endurance." If you've come into this training with a year of consistent weight training under your belt, make these the "Power" workouts described below. If not, then weight training is relatively new for you. We suggest sticking with the complete "Endurance" weight workouts.

Speed of Execution: Explosive yet controlled concentric lifts and slow eccentric lowering—two seconds to lift and four seconds to lower weight. When doing sets of 15, think speed, even on endurance exercises.

Resistance: Split the exercises into two groups. Half will be performed in the medium to heavy intensity range: 2-3 sets of 4-8 reps with weight loads of 85-90% of estimated maximum. The remaining exercises will be in the medium range resistance like in the Endurance phase: the same 2-3 sets of 15 reps. The exercises that you "Power" on Thursday become endurance exercises on Sunday, and vice-versa for the Thursday Endurance exercises.

4. CHISEL (WEEKS 17-20)

Purpose: This phase can translate strength into power (or strength applied quickly). Drop all leg exercises except the lunges—save your energy for the miles on the road.

Speed of Execution: Think SPEED, even in rests. Take two seconds to lift, two seconds to lower (remember to think control!).

Resistance: Light to medium range. Two sets of 10-12 repetitions.

ORDER OF EXERCISES

If your time management program is starting to crack, do only the highlighted exercises.

STRENGTH TRAINING EXERCISES

(Listed in the order to be performed)

1. Warm-up
2. Total body warm-up
3. Robot arms
4. Squats / leg press
5. Lat. Pull-down
6. Leg extension
7. Bench press
8. Leg curl
9. Dumbbell pullover
10. Walking or reverse lunges
11. Seated / Upright rows
12. Straight biceps curls
13. Calf raises
14. Supinated biceps curls
15. Anterior tibs
16. Triceps extensions, with rope or kick backs
17. Lateral raises (deltoids)
18. Standing abduction and adduction
19. Back extension
20. Abdominals
21. Press-ups
22. Stretch

Strength training is the cornerstone of an optimal Ironman performance.

CHAPTER 5
Adaptation Phase
Weeks 1-6

The focus of this first six-week program is on strength training and getting into a "training groove." While it's impossible to not think about the fact that you have an Ironman race in 24 weeks, your specific physical preparation won't begin for another 14 weeks. As anxious as you might be to start doing long runs and rides, realize that starting Ironman-specific training right now will only lead to injury and mental burnout. You need to install the physical plumbing and framework necessary to handle the increased stress such training will incur. That's what this first six-week stretch is about.

Some of you may already be in good or even great shape in one or two of the three disciplines. If, for example, you've been in a consistent running program and are doing weekend road races, that's fine. You can continue to do this while bringing the other two sports up to par as prescribed in this program. In other words, you don't have to go backwards with your training. You can simply maintain the fitness you've already achieved.

It's okay to move workouts around to suit your life and local training schedule. If you have a group long run on Saturday and like to ride on Sunday, switch these two days in the program. One simple rule: while it's okay to put a swim workout on the same day as a quality or long bike or run, DO NOT have a long or hard bike on the same day as a long or hard run.

If you want to "jump start" your weakest discipline, you can add one to two workouts per week in that weakness. However! If you do this you must make room for the additional time spent by eliminating one or two workouts in the other disciplines. For example, perhaps you're a great cyclist with years of experience but sink like a rock in the water. You can skip (or shorten) the Tuesday bike workout and do a swim workout instead.

Let those around you know what's going on. This first six weeks of training won't be as time and energy-consuming as what comes later, so it's a good time to get your immediate family and circle of friends used to the idea and make plans to handle your increased workload and decreased availability.

Friday, during the first three weeks, is a complete day off and will become an optional day off starting week four. Some people love having a complete day off from training, while others will go crazy. Here is the rule to live by: If you can truly perform an easy session or two on a day off and keep the heart rate and effort very low, feeling refreshed afterwards, then it is okay. If you find yourself going that five or ten heartbeats harder then you should, force yourself to sleep in Friday morning and sit on the sofa Friday night.

This is an appropriate time to add running drills and accelerations, preferably at the end of one of your easier runs (when your legs aren't fatigued from a hard workout but are thoroughly warmed up). Starting in week four, these are scheduled at the end of your track/intensity run workouts, but you can keep doing them on the easy run days. If you know you won't do them in an unstructured environment (easy run days), however, go ahead and do them at the end of your key run day (the intensity/track workout).

SWIM WORKOUTS FOR ADAPTATION PHASE

The focus in the water for the first six weeks should be on technique, with one workout solely devoted to this. Below is the freestyle drill progression that will be used during the Monday technique swim sessions.

TERMS

If you come across any workouts, training techniques or shorthand that you don't get, check back with Chapter Two for a thorough description.

WEEK #1: BUILD

MONDAY

Swim 3,000 yd Technique workout		
Warm-up:	200 freestyle	
	100 kick	
	200 freestyle	
	100 kick all with 15-20 seconds rest	
Main set:	Freestyle drills	
	All done with 10-15 seconds rest between each 50	
	100 kicking on your stomach, arms at your side	
	5-10 x 50 as:	25 kick on left side
		25 kick on right side
	Concentrate on keeping your hips up; keep your chin, cheek or ear into your shoulder except when breathing. This kick drill is done completely on your side.	
	5-10 x 50 S2S kicking drill	
	Rotate from one side to the other every 6-9 kicks	
	5-10 x 50 as:	25 left arm
		25 right arm
	5-10 x 50 C/U	
Cool-down:	200 Cheating C/U swimming	
	Concentrate on doing the stroke the way we want to see it	
	100 choice easy	

© iStockphoto/Thinkstock

TUESDAY

Bike 70 minute turbo workout

Warm up		
Main Set:	3 x 3 minutes as:	20 seconds fast spin
		40 seconds easy
		40 seconds fast spin
		20 seconds easy
		1 minute fast spin
		1 minute easy
	6 x 3 minutes as:	3 x (45 seconds at <100 RPM 15 sec <100 RPM) at HR#2
	2 minutes easy spin after each 3 minute interval	
Cool-down:	10 minutes easy spin	

Run 15-20 minute transition run (T-run) performed after your bike intervals (within 10 minutes) at an easy effort of HR#1-2

WEDNESDAY

Key Swim 3,500 yd aerobic workout

Warm-up:	24 x 50 as:	2 freestyle
		2 stroke *on 10 seconds rest*
Main set:	10 x 150 as:	50 freestyle
		50 stroke
		50 freestyle easy *on 15 seconds rest*
Cool-down:	8 x 75 as:	3 kick
		3 drill
		2 choice *on 15 seconds rest*

Optional Bike 60-90 minute easy ride at HR#1-2

THURSDAY

Swim 2,500 yd Sprint workout

Warm-up:	4 x 200 as:	2 freestyle
		1 kick
		1 stroke *all on 15 seconds rest*
	9 x 50 as:	3 stroke on 15 seconds rest
		3 freestyle on 10 seconds rest
		3 freestyle on 5 seconds rest
Main set:	3 x 100 fast (80-90%) on 20 seconds rest	
	2 x 75 easy choice on 20 seconds rest	
	6 x 100 freestyle as:	2 on 20 seconds rest easy (HR#1)
		2 on 15 seconds rest moderate (HR#2)
		2 on 10 seconds rest somewhat hard (HR#3)
Cool-down:	200 easy choice	

Key Run Fartlek

Warm-up:	15-20 minutes at easy to moderate pace.
Main set:	15-20 minutes of fartlek with 3-6 x 45 second pickups
	Just up the tempo a bit, not anywhere close to a wide out sprint. Run for 2-3 minutes easy between each pickup.
Cool-down:	15-20 minutes easy to moderate running

Weights 30-60 minutes, light. 1 x 10 reps per set

FRIDAY

Off

SATURDAY

Swim Optional 30 minute easy swim.

Best performed before the long bike ride or later in the day after the bike and run.

Key Bike 2-3 hour long ride at HR#1

Run 15-20 transition run at HR#1

SUNDAY

Run 50-70 minute long run at HR#1

Weights Same as Thursday

© iStockphoto/Thinkstock

WEEK #2: BUILD

MONDAY

Swim Technique workout		
Warm-up:	500 freestyle	
	200 choice	
	300 kick-swim by the 50	
Main set:	2 x (1 x 400) as:	25 kick on stomach w/arms at side
		25 kick on left, 25 kick on right, 25 S2S
	Four times through. Take 1 minute rest, then:	
	1 x 400 as:	50 C/U
		50 Cheating C/U
	Four times through with 30 seconds rest	
Cool-down:	200-400 choice easy	

TUESDAY

Bike 70-minute turbo workout		
Warm-up:	15-20 minutes spinning easy to moderate	
	with single leg drills (SLD)	
Main set:	2 x 20 second SLD, 40 seconds both legs	
	then 30 second SLD, 30 seconds both legs	
	40 second SLD, 20 seconds both legs	
	50 second SLD/ 10 seconds both legs	
	All in small chain ring and easy gear at ----> 80RPM	
	4 x 5 minutes as:	2 minutes in big gear seated at < 80RPM
		1 minute fast spin at > 100RPM
		2 minutes again in big gear standing
	All at HR #2 mid to high, with 2 minutes easy spin after each 5 minute interval	
Cool-down:	10-15 minutes easy to moderate spin	
Run 15-20 minute T-run performed after your bike intervals (within 10 minutes) at HR#1-2		

WEDNESDAY

Key Swim Aerobic workout

Warm-up:	500 freestyle	
	10 x 50 drill or stroke on 10 seconds rest	
Main set:	15 x 100 pull easy on 15 seconds rest	
	20 x 50 as:	1 kick on side
		1 stroke on 10 seconds rest easy
Cool-down:	500 easy choice	

Bike Optional 60-90 minute easy ride at HR#1-2

THURSDAY

Swim Sprint workout

Warm-up:	6 x 150 freestyle easy on 20 seconds rest	
Main set:	16 x 100 as:	2 freestyle moderate (HR#2-3)
		1 Individual Medley (IM) easy *all on 20 seconds rest*
		3 x 200 pull easy on 30 seconds rest
Cool-down:	4 x 100 as:	50 drill
	50 stroke *on 10 seconds rest, easy*	

Key Run Fartlek

Warm-up:	15-20 minutes easy to moderate
Main set:	15-20 minutes fartlek
	with 3-6 x 1-minute pickups
	at HR#2 high to HR#3 low
	Just up the tempo a bit, not anywhere close to a hard sprint. Same as last week but just a little longer with 2-3 minutes easy running between.
Cool-down:	15-20 minutes easy to moderate

Weights Keep the weight very light again this second week and perform 1 x 12 reps of each exercise

FRIDAY

Off

SATURDAY

Swim Optional easy 30 minutes.

Best to be performed before the long bike ride or later in the day after the bike and run.

Key Bike 2-3 hour long ride at HR#1

Run 15-20 transition run at HR#1

SUNDAY

Bike Optional 60 minute ride at HR#1

Run 60-80 minute long run at HR#1

Weights Same as Thursday

WEEK #3: RECOVERY

MONDAY

Swim Technique workout		
Warm-up:	300 freestyle	
	100 kick	
	300 choice	
	100 kick	
Main set:	10 x 100 as:	25 kick on stomach w/arms at side
		25 S2S
		25 C/U
		25 freestyle
		all with 20 seconds rest between each
	4 x 200 pull or swim easy	
	with 20 seconds rest between each	
Cool-down:	12 x 50 easy as:	25 kick on stomach, arms out front
		25 swim choice on 15 seconds rest

TUESDAY

Bike 70-minute turbo trainer workout		
Warm-up:	15-20 minutes easy to moderate	
Main set:	8-10 x 30 seconds fast spin at > 100RPM	
	with 30 seconds easy between each burst	
	Try to make each 30 seconds interval progressively faster.	
	5-6 x 4 minutes as:	2 x (1:30 fast spin at > 100RPM in an easy gear
		30 seconds big gear standing or seated
		Aim for high HR#2-low HR#3
		2 minutes easy after each 4 minutes
Cool-down:	10-15 minutes easy to moderate spin	
Run 15-20 minute T-run at HR#1-2		

WEDNESDAY

Key Swim Aerobic workout	
Warm-up:	6 x 50 freestyle on 10 seconds rest
	200 drill freestyle (catch-up or layout freestyle)
Main set:	600 freestyle
	6 x 100 freestyle
	400 freestyle
	8 x 50 freestyle
	400 freestyle
	16 x 25 freestyle
	All aerobic with 10-30 seconds rest
Cool-down:	6 x 50 as:

		25 drill
Cool-down:	6 x 50 as:	25 drill
		25 choice on 10 seconds rest

THURSDAY

Key Run	
Warm-up:	15-20 minutes easy to moderate running
Main set:	15-20 minutes fartlek
	with 3-6 x 90 second pickups
	This is simply a progression on the last two weeks intervals. Perform the pickups at HR#2-high to HR#3-low with 2-3 minutes easy running between.
Cool-down:	15-20 minutes at easy to moderate pace

Weights 1 x 15 reps of each exercise

Once again, keep the weights very light.

FRIDAY

Off

SATURDAY

Swim Optional easy 30 minute swim of your choice.

Key Bike 1.5-2 hours at HR#1

Run Because the focus in on recovery, no T-run this Saturday.

SUNDAY

Run 50-70 minute long run at HR#1

Weights Same as Thursday

WEEK #4: TESTING

MONDAY

Swim Test *See Chapter 2, p. 24 for instructions, or do workout below.*

Warm-up:	4 x 300 as:	1 freestyle
		1 kick
		1 choice
		1 pull
Main set:	10-16 x 25 as:	1 kick on side (1/2 length on each side)
		1 S2S
		1 C/U
		1 swim, *all with 5 seconds rest after each*
	Easy 500 freestyle	
	1 minute rest	
	10-16 x 25 as:	1 kick on side (1/2 length on each side)
		1 S2S
		1 C/U
		1 swim *all with 5 seconds rest after each*
	then swim easy 400 freestyle	
	1 minute rest	
	10-16 x 25 as:	1 kick on side (1/2 length on each side)
		1 S2S
		1 C/U
		1 swim *all with 5 seconds rest after each*
Cool-down:	300 choice easy	

TUESDAY

Bike Test *See Chapter 2, p. 24 for instructions.*
Run 15-20 minute T-run at HR#1-2

WEDNESDAY

Key Swim *Test! See Chapter 2, p. 24 for instructions.*

Warm-up:	8 x 100 choice on 15 seconds rest	
Main set:	1500 straight as:	150 easy
		50 moderate to hard
	6 x 150 as:	50 easy
		50 moderate to hard
		50 easy on 20 seconds rest
Cool-down:	12 x 25 as:	1 fast
		3 easy on 15 seconds rest

Bike 60-90 minutes easy ride at HR#1

THURSDAY

Key Run Intervals

This run can be performed on the road, trails or track.	
Warm-up:	15-20 minutes easy to moderate with 4 accelerations
Main set:	8/7/6/5 minutes
	all steady at HR#2-high to #3-low
	with 3 minute recovery jog after each effort
	These runs should be 10-15 beats below AT or just starting to hit a somewhat hard effort, something close to your race pace for a half-marathon. This should NOT be anywhere near a maximum effort. Think control. If you're dreading this workout, you're going way too hard.
Cool-down:	15-20 minutes jog followed by stretching
	If you are not running on Fridays and have NOT performed your drills and accelerations at the end of your Tuesday transition run, then perform them before you do your cool-down run.

Weights Keep it controlled and light while increasing to 2 x 12 this week.

This day is optional. If you're tired or time strapped, you can take it off.

Swim Sprint session		
Warm-up:	2 x	
	4 x 50 freestyle	
	1 x 100 IM	
	1 x 100 freestyle all on 10 seconds rest	
	12 x 25 as:	1 kick
		2 drill
		1 freestyle on 10 seconds rest
Main set:	200 freestyle (HR#2)	
	50 fast (HR#3-4)	
	200 freestyle (HR#2)	
	100 fast (HR#3-4)	
	200 freestyle (HR#2)	
	150 fast (HR#3-4)	
	200 freestyle (HR#2)	
	200 fast (HR#3-4) *all on 20-30 seconds rest*	
Cool-down:	300 kick	
	200 pull	
	100 drill	
	100 choice *all easy on 10-20 seconds rest*	

Bike 60 minute easy ride at HR#1

Run 30-50 minutes at HR #1 with drills and accelerations at end

SATURDAY

Swim Optional easy 30 minute swim of your choice

Key Bike 120-180 minute long ride at HR#1

Run 20 minute T-run at HR#1-2

SUNDAY

Bike Optional 60 minute easy ride at HR#1

Run 70-90 minute long run at HR#1-2

Weights Same as Thursday

© iStockphoto/Thinkstock

WEEK #5: BUILD/TESTING

MONDAY

Swim Technique workout		
Warm-up:	500 Freestyle	
	5 x 100 as:	100 choice
		100 K/S freestyle *on 15 seconds rest*
Main set:	200 as:	50 kick on side (25 on each side)
		50 C/U – 100 swim with 30 seconds rest after
		5-8 x 100 freestyle moderate on 10 seconds rest
	200 as:	50 kick on side (25 on each side)
		50 C/U
		100 swim *with 30 seconds rest*
	4-6 x 100 freestyle moderate on 10 seconds rest	
	200 as:	50 kick on side (25 on each side)
		50 C/U
		100 swim with 30 seconds rest
	2-4 x 100 freestyle moderate on 10 seconds rest	
Cool-down:	4-8 x 25 choice easy on 5 seconds rest	

TUESDAY

Bike 70 minute turbo workout			
Warm-up:	15-20 minutes easy to moderate		
Main set:	4 x 30 seconds fast spin		
	30 seconds easy		
	Then we'll do a ladder:	1/2/3/4/5/4/3/2/1 minutes	
		all at HR#2-3 low with 2 minutes easy	
		between each interval	
	Try to keep your RPM at 90+ and stay in the aero position as much as possible.		
	3 x 40 seconds SLD		
	20 seconds left leg		
	20 seconds right leg		
	20 seconds both legs		
Cool-down:	10-15 minutes easy to moderate spin		
Run 15-20 minute T-run at HR#1-2			

WEDNESDAY

Key Swim Anaerobic Threshold session

Warm-up:	8 x 100 as	4 freestyle
		4 choice *all on 20 seconds rest*
Main set:	8-10 x 200 steady at 80-85% (hr#2-3) effort on 20 seconds rest	
Cool-down:	500-700 choice easy	

THURSDAY

Key Run Test *See Chapter 3 for instructions.*

Weights Increase to 2 x 15 this week. Keep it light.

FRIDAY

Again, this is an optional day of training.

Swim Sprint session

Warm-up:	100 freestyle	
	200 choice	
	300 freestyle	
	400 Rev IM all easy on 15 seconds rest	
	12x 25 as:	1 kick choice no board
		1 stroke *on 10 seconds rest*
Main set:	2-3 x 200 as:	25 stroke
		75 freestyle at HR#2
		30 seconds rest
		4 x 50 descend 1-4 to max effort
		on 15 seconds rest
		8 x 25 freestyle stroke drills on 10 seconds rest
Cool-down:	3 x 100 as:	2 pull
		1 choice easy *on 10 seconds rest*
Bike 60 minute easy ride at HR#1		
Run 30-50 minutes at HR#1 with drills and accelerations at end		

SATURDAY

Swim Optional easy 30 minute swim of your choice

Key Bike 150-210 minute long ride at HR#1

Run 20 minute T-run at HR#1-2

SUNDAY

Bike Optional 60 minute easy ride at HR#1

Run 80-100 minute long run at HR#1-2

Weights Same as Thursday

© iStockphoto/Thinkstock

WEEK #6: RECOVERY

MONDAY

Swim Technique workout			
Warm-up:	600 Freestyle		
	200 kick		
	200 choice		
	all with 20-30 seconds rest between sets		
Main set:	12 x 75 as:	25 kick on side (1/2 length on each side)	
		25 C/U	
		25 freestyle with 15 seconds rest after each	
	6 x 200 freestyle easy to moderate		
	on 20 seconds rest		
Cool-down:	4-8 x 50 choice on 10 seconds rest		

TUESDAY

Bike Turbo session	
Warm-up:	15-20 minutes of easy to moderate riding
Main set:	4-6 x 4 minutes fast spin
	45 seconds easy
	2-3 x 5 minutes steady at HR#2
	with cadence 95RPM+
	2 minutes easy

	9-15 minutes Roller Coaster as:	1 minute in a big gear seated or standing
		at HR#2
		1 minute fast spin also at HR#2
		1 minute fast at HR#3

	2 x 10 seconds fast spinning jumps
	1:50 easy spin after each
	To perform fast spin jumps, shift into an easy gear and get your RPM up to a normal 85-95, then for 15 seconds spin as fast as you can without falling off the bike, then 1:45 easy back at a regular cadence. Stay seated throughout the jumps and try not to bounce.
	2x 10 seconds big gear jumps
	1:50 easy spin after each
	Very similar to fast spinning jumps, but start in a very big gear at a slow cadence of <50RPM. For 10 seconds stay seated and power very hard to get up to speed while keeping the upper body quiet and working only from the hips down, then shift into an easy gear and spin for 1:50.
Cool-down:	10-15 minutes easy to moderate spin

Run 15-20 minute T-run at HR#1-2, performed within 10 minutes of finishing the turbo workout

WEDNESDAY

Key Swim Aerobic workout		
Warm-up:	10 x 25 freestyle	
	4 x 50 choice	
	2 x 100 as:	50 freestyle
		50 choice *all on 10-15 seconds rest*
	8 x 50 as:	25 single arm freestyle
		25 back on 10 seconds rest
Main set:	50/150/250/350/450/350/250/150/50	
	All aerobic freestyle with the first 50 always stroke and 10-20 seconds rest between all	
Cool-down:	12 x 25 as:	1 back
		1 freestyle *on 10 seconds rest*

THURSDAY

Key Run Key Workout	
Warm-up:	15-20 minutes easy to moderate,
Main set:	20-30 minutes moderate run
	with 5-7 x 1-minute pick-ups at HR#2-3
	3 minutes easy between each
	Drills and accelerations
Cool-down:	15-20 minutes easy to moderate.
Weights 2 x 15 reps of each exercise at a light weight	

FRIDAY

Off

SATURDAY

Swim Optional easy 30 minute swim of your choice
Key Bike 120-180 minute long ride at HR#1
Run 20 minute T-run at HR#1-2

SUNDAY

Bike Optional 60 minute easy ride at HR#1

Run 60-80 minute long run at HR#1-2

Weights Same as Thursday

QUESTIONS & ANSWERS

Q: I'm having trouble completing some of the swim workouts in less than 90 minutes. Is there some way to cut them short?

A: Adjust swim sessions + or − 1,000 yards depending on your current swimming ability. To adjust the workouts, simply add or delete 100-200 yards from all the sets.

Q: How flexible is this schedule?

A: You can allow yourself some flexibility during this first six weeks, as you get back into the groove of a regimented training schedule. There are NO "have to's" during this first six weeks except for lifting twice a week and getting in at least one swim, bike and run each week. However, starting with the second six-week phase, we recommend that you be as consistent as possible with the training we prescribe.

Q: I have the prescribed triathlon background, but I'm coming into this program after a layoff. Is that okay?

A: If you have been dormant for the past few months and this is the start to your training comeback, then be very careful with the amount of training that you perform each week. Only do the "key" workouts and perform the lower range of the sessions at a very low intensity. As you start to feel better, increase the duration of these key sessions each week before you add more sessions. Remember that your race is not for another 24 weeks. Ease back into your training and let your body get fit slowly rather than rushing it.

CHAPTER 6
Aerobic Phase
Weeks 7-12

The focus of this second 6-week program is still on strength training. That said, you should be firmly into a training routine and starting to feel like a triathlete again.

You should be up to two sets of 15 repetitions in the gym (see the "Endurance Phase" in Chapter 4: Weight Training). Now you need to pay attention to the hard/easy aspect when you get to the last two to three repetitions of each set. You should feel fatigued, but able to perform one more rep after the 15th. If it is beginning to feel easy (you should be making some strength gains), simply add a little weight.

The following still applies: It's okay to move workouts around to suit your schedule. If you have a group long run on Saturday and like to ride on Sunday, switch these two days in the program. We repeat: while it's okay to put a swim workout on the same day as a bike or run, try to NOT have a long or hard bike on the same day as a long or hard run.

Remember how in the last program we said it was okay to skip a workout here and there? That time is over. You need to begin to get consistent with the key workouts (key workouts are underlined for easy identification) at the minimum! This doesn't mean you should train through illness/injury, but simply that it's time to get serious about training for something known as an Ironman.

We've scheduled an optional day off on Fridays (some might find this fits better on Mondays) and a recovery week. These are as important as the training. If you can't do ONE (and no, we don't expect you to do all three) of the EASY workouts suggested on Friday and feel recovered afterward, DON'T do it! The key on the recovery week is to decrease BOTH the intensity and duration of all workouts. You need the recovery week to digest the hard training in the weeks leading up to it.

Group workouts are fine but don't turn them into races. Especially on the Saturday long rides and Sunday long runs, don't go too hard – these are meant

to be performed at a relatively EASY intensity. Leave high intensity days for Tuesdays and Thursdays.

Running drills and accelerations have been scheduled at the end of your Thursday intensity run workouts, but are best done at the end of one of your easier runs (when your legs aren't fatigued from a hard workout but are warmed up). If you know you won't do them in an unstructured environment (easy run days), go ahead and do them at the end of your Thursday key run sessions.

Transition runs (T-runs) need to be kept on the easy / moderate side of intensity right now. Also remember that these don't need to be a pit-stop at a NASCAR race. It's okay to allow yourself time to get changed, get a drink and something to eat, or go to the bathroom before the run. Just don't settle into the recliner in front of Oprah and let an hour whiz by.

We have not scheduled in training time for flexibility, but are assuming that everyone will take at least 15 minutes twice a week to work on a range of motions. Try to perform stretches at the end of a training session as you will be warmed up. Better yet, schedule in a yoga session twice a week if time permits. You can get away with a limited range of motion when you are young (25 years or under), but you can not fake it after that.

WEEK #7: BUILD

MONDAY

Swim Technique session	
Warm-up:	400 free
	100 kick
	200 free
	100 kick *all with 15 seconds rest*
Main set:	18 x 50
	Odd 25 S2S drill – 25 C/U, even free swim on 15 seconds rest
	3 x 500 free swim, even pace
	1 minute rest after each
Cool-down:	300 choice easy

TUESDAY

Key Bike 70-minute turbo workout	
Warm-up:	15-20 minutes easy to moderate
Main set:	5 x 45 seconds fast spin
	45 seconds easy
	increase RPM's every 15 seconds
	6 x 3 minutes big gear intervals
	alternating one standing/one seated
	all at HR#2-high to HR#3-low
	2 minutes easy after each
	10 minutes steady at HR#2
	at 100RPM-plus cadence in aero position
	2 x 10 seconds fast spinning jumps
	1:50 easy spin after each
	To perform, shift into an easy gear and get your cadence up to a normal 85-95, then for 15 seconds spin as fast as you can without falling off the bike, then 1:45 easy back at a regular cadence. Focus on staying seated, keeping the upper body quiet and trying not to bounce. Relax from the hips down.

	2 x 10 seconds Big Gear jumps
	1:50 easy spin after each
	Very similar to fast spinning jumps, but start in a very big gear at a very slow cadence of <50RPM. For 10 seconds stay seated and power very hard to get up to speed while keeping the upper body quiet and working only from the hips down, then shift into an easy gear and spin for 1:50.
Cool-down:	10-15 minutes easy to moderate spin

Key Run A 15-20 minute transition run (T-run) performed after your bike intervals (within 10 minutes) at an easy effort of HR#1-2

WEDNESDAY

Key Swim Aerobic session

Warm-up:	5 x 200 as:	2 freestyle
		1 kick
		2 choice *on 20 seconds rest*
Main set:	4 x 500 as:	alternating 1-500 straight on 30 seconds rest
		1-5 x 100 on 10 seconds rest *all at 85% (HR#3)*
Cool-down:	5 x 100 as:	1 freestyle
		1 kick
		1 pull
		1 drill
		1 freestyle *on 10 seconds rest*

Optional Bike 60-90 minute easy ride at HR#1-2

Key Run Fartlek			
Warm-up:	20 minutes easy to moderate and stretch		
	2nd warm-up of 10 minutes with 4 accelerations		
Main set:	36 minutes fartlek on track, road or trail as:		
	3 x	1 minute on/1 off	
		3 on/1 off	
		5 on/1 off	
	All "on" at HR#2-3, 15km-half marathon pace and then "off" easy jog at HR#1.		
	2 x 20-40 drills of each and 6 x accelerations		
	Do these only if you have not done them on Tuesday or don't plan to do them on Friday		
Cool-down:	10-15 minutes easy to moderate and stretch		
Weights 30-60 minutes, 2 x 15 reps per set			
See "Endurance Phase" in Chapter 4.			

FRIDAY

Optional day off

Swim Sprint session		
Warm-up:	4 x 150 (3 freestyle/1 kick) on 10 seconds rest	
Main set:	30 x 25 as:	10 stroke easy
		10 freestyle moderate
		10 freestyle on faster interval
	The last 10 freestyle should be fast on a 10 seconds rest interval	
	20 x 50 as:	5 IM easy on 15 seconds rest
	15 freestyle:	first 5 moderate on 15 seconds rest
		next 5 faster on 10 seconds rest
		last 5 very fast on 5 seconds rest
Cool-down:	Easy 200 choice	
Bike 60 minute easy ride at HR#1		

Run 30-50 minute easy run HR#1. Drills and accelerations

For both the bike and run, only do it if you can do it easy and feel recovered afterwards. 30-50 minutes easy at HR#1 with drills and accelerations at end if you didn't do them Tuesday or Thursday.

IT'S VERY IMPORTANT to get in your drills and accelerations once a week, year round! You should already be up to 40 to 60 steps of each drill and 6 to 8 x 100 meter accelerations. If not, start with 2 x 20 reps of all three drills (high knees, butt kicks, skipping) and add 5-10 reps each week, building up to 2 sets of 50-60 reps. Start with 4 accelerations and add 1-2 each week, building up to as many as 16.

SATURDAY

Swim Optional 30-45 minutes easy swim.

Best to be performed before the long bike ride or later in the day after the bike and run.

Key Bike 3-4 hour long ride at HR#2

Key Run 15-20 transition run (T-run) at HR#1

SUNDAY

Key Run 80-100 minute long run at HR#2

Weights Same as Thursday

WEEK #8: BUILD

MONDAY

Swim Technique

Warm-up:	2 x	300 freestyle
		200 choice
		100 IM *on 15 seconds rest*
Main set:	16 x 25 as:	25 left arm
		25 right arm
		25 C/U
		25 C/U) *all easy on 5 seconds rest*
	8 x 200 freestyle easy aerobic even pace on 15-20 seconds rest	
Cool-down:	8 x 50 as:	2 freestyle
		2 stroke
		2 kick
		2 choice easy *on 10-15 seconds rest*

TUESDAY

Key Bike 70-minute turbo workout **Big Gear Intervals**	
Warm-up:	15-20 minutes gradual warm-up
	4 x 30 seconds SLD
	30 seconds both legs
	4 x 40 seconds fast spin
	20 seconds easy
Main set:	4 x 5 minutes Big Gear with 2 minutes easy
	After each, keep heart rate no higher than low HR#3. Alternate every 30 seconds between seated and standing on #1 and #3. #2 and #4 your choice of seated or standing.
	3 x 20 seconds SLD in bigger gear
	40 seconds both legs
	3 x 10 seconds fast spinning jumps
	1:50 easy spin after each
	To perform, shift into an easy gear and get your RPM up to a normal 85-95, then for 15 seconds spin as fast as you can without falling off the bike, then 1:45 easy back at a regular cadence. Stay seated and keep the upper body quiet, trying not to bounce.
	3 x 10 seconds Big Gear jumps
	1:50 easy spin after each
	Very similar to fast spinning jumps, but start in a very big gear at a very slow cadence of <50RPM. For 10 seconds stay seated and power very hard to get up to speed while keeping the upper body quiet and working only from the hips down, then shift into an easy gear and spin for 1:50.
Cool-down:	10-15 minutes gradual cool down
Key Run 20-30 minute T-run performed after your bike intervals (within 10 minutes) at HR#1-2	

WEDNESDAY

Key Swim Anaerobic session

Warm-up:	400 freestyle	
	300 stroke	
	200 freestyle *all on 30 seconds rest*	
	6x 100 as:	25 kick
		50 drill
		25 kick *on 15 seconds rest*
Main set:	2 x 200	
	3 x 100	
	2 x 200	
	3 x 100 *all at 85% (HR#3) on 10-20 seconds rest*	
Cool-down:	12 x 50 as:	3 kick
		3 drill
		3 freestyle
		3 stroke *all easy on 15 seconds rest*

Bike Optional 60-90 minute easy ride at HR#1-2

THURSDAY

Key Run Track intervals

Warm-up:	20 minutes and stretch
	6 x accelerations
Main set:	1/2/3/4/5 laps on a 400m track
	Descend from marathon pace for the first 1 lapper (HR#2 high) to 10km pace (HR#3 high) on the 5 lapper, all with 400 moderate jog between. If not on the track, this workout can be performed on the road or trails as follows: 2/4/6/8/10 minutes descending effort from HR#2 high on the 10 minutes to HR#3 high on the 2 minutes. 2 minutes easy jog between each interval. If you're not conservative early, the last effort (the 5-lap or 10 minutes) will be brutal. Keep the focus of the workout on getting faster!
	2 x 20-40 drills of each
	Add in 8-10 x accelerations if you have not done these on Tuesday or plan to do on Friday.

Cool-down:	10-15 minutes gradual cool-down and stretch
Weights 30-60 minutes, light, 2 x 15 reps per set	
See "Endurance Phase" in Chapter 4.	

FRIDAY

Optional day off. Do as many – or as few – of the workouts you feel up for.

Swim Sprint session		
Warm-up:	300 freestyle	
	3 x 100 freestyle on 10 seconds rest 200 IM	
	4x 100 as:	50 kick
		50 freestyle on 15 seconds rest
Main set:	8 x 75 fast on 30 seconds rest	
Cool-down:	300 choice	
Bike 60 minute easy ride at HR#1		
Run 30-50 minute easy run HR#1. Drills and strides at the end of the run		

SATURDAY

Swim Optional easy 30 minutes
While maintaining swimming frequency is important to improving "feel" for the water, at the end of this week you might be tired. So don't swim if you think it's going to push you over the edge.
Key Bike 210-270 minute long ride at HR#2
Key Run 15-20 transition run at HR#1-2

SUNDAY

Bike Easy 60-90 minutes ride at HR#1
If you can't do this ride easy, then score some points at home and mow the lawn or wash the windows. Or just settle in with the morning paper.
Key Run 90-105 minute long run at HR#2.
You know the deal – it's about spending time on your legs – NOT going hard. Keep it aerobic.
Weights Same as Thursday

WEEK #9: RECOVERY

MONDAY

Swim Technique session

Warm-up:	5 x 200 as:	1 freestyle
		1 kick
		1 pull
		1 kick
		1 choice *all with 15-20 seconds rest*
Main set:	6 x 100 freestyle drills as:	25 S2S
		50 C/U
		25 freestyle *all on 15 rest between each*
	600 Freestyle easy to moderate	
	1 minute rest	
	4 x 100 freestyle drills as:	25 S2S
		50 C/U
		25 freestyle *all on 15 rest between each*
	400 Freestyle easy to moderate	
	1 minute rest	
	2 x 100 freestyle drills as:	25 S2S
		50 C/U
		25 freestyle *all on 15 rest between each*
Cool-down:	400 easy choice	

TUESDAY

Key Bike 70-minute turbo workout **Big Gear Intervals**	
Warm-up:	15-20 minutes gradual warm-up
Main set:	2 x 8 minutes
	Build one gear harder every 2 minutes to a max of HR#2 on first set and HR#3-low on second set. Adjust cadence to keep heart rate in range. 2 minutes easy between sets.
	Down the ladder
	Starting with a 5-minute interval, go 5/4/3/2/1-minutes in a large gear with the last 1 minute a fast spin at HR#2-3. 2 minutes easy between each hard effort.
	2 x 15 seconds fast spinning jumps
	1:45 easy spin after each
	2 x 15 seconds Big Gear jumps
	1:45 easy spin after each
Cool-down:	10-15 minutes gradual cool-down
Key Run 20-30 minute T-run at HR#1-2	
Perform this within 10 minutes of finishing the turbo workout.	

WEDNESDAY

Key Swim Aerobic session	
Warm-up:	100 freestyle
	200 drill
	300 freestyle
	400 IM
	8 x 25 kick easy on 10 seconds rest
	2 x 200 pull easy on 20 seconds rest
Main set:	3 x
	2 x 150 on 15 seconds rest easy
	6 x 50 easy on 10 seconds rest
Cool-down:	300 choice
Bike 60 minute easy ride at HR#1	
Only if time and energy is available.	

THURSDAY

Key Run Fartlek	
Warm-up:	20 minutes and stretch
Main set:	30-40 minutes of fartlek running
	This is a "run-how-you-feel" workout: Knock out what intervals you feel like doing while keeping within heart #1-#3-low
	2x 20-40 drills of each and 10-12x accelerations
	Do these only if you have not done these on Tuesday or are not planning to do them on Friday.
Cool-down:	10-15 minutes gradual cool-down and stretch

Weights 2 x 15 reps light to medium Endurance phase
Only increase weight in the exercises where your last 2 to 3 repetitions of each set are feeling easy (like you could still do 3 more after #15). The Endurance Phase's main purpose is to increase strength levels and muscular endurance. It is very important to keep the speed and execution of all exercises slow and controlled. Keep the number of reps and sets the same over the next six weeks and increase the weight as needed. Remember: You should always be able to complete all sets and reps. Never go to failure. Refer to Chapter 4 for further information on this phase.

FRIDAY

Off

SATURDAY

Swim Optional easy 30 minute swim of your choice.
Since it's recovery week, you should be a bit more rested by now (the weekend). If not, skip this easy swim. If you're rested, this is a great opportunity to give your swimming the boost of an additional day in the water.

Key Bike 2-3 hours at HR#1-2
Key Run 15-20 minute T-run at HR#1-2

SUNDAY

Bike Optional 60 minutes easy at HR#1

Key Run 60-80 minute long run at HR#1-2

Weights Same as Thursday

WEEK #10: BUILD

MONDAY

Swim Technique session

Warm-up:	2 x 300 freestyle
	200 choice which means any stroke, kick, or drill of your choice *all on 20-30 seconds rest*
Main set:	10 x 50 freestyle easy
	10 seconds rest between each
	500 freestyle easy to moderate with 1 minute rest after
	400 kick-swim as:
	200 K/S same as the 400
	Finish with a perfect 100 freestyle
Cool-down:	12 x 25 choice on 5 seconds rest easy

The "400 kick-swim as:" block contains:

| 50 kick |
| 50 swim *with 30 seconds rest* |
| 300 freestyle easy to moderate |
| with 1 minute rest after |

TUESDAY

Key Bike Turbo workout **Fast Spinning**

Warm-up:	15-20 minutes gradual warm-up
	3 x 45 minutes SLD
	45 seconds both legs
	6 x 20 seconds fast spin
	40 seconds easy
	2 x 45 minutes SLD
	45 seconds both legs
Main set:	2 x 5/3/1 minute steady at mid-HR#3
	1 minute easy between, *all seated 95RPM or greater in aero position*
	3 x 15 seconds fast spinning jumps
	1:45 easy spin after each
	1 x 15 seconds Big Gear jumps
	1:45 easy spin after each
Cool-down:	10-15 minutes gradual cool-down

Key Run 20-30 minute T-run at HR#1-2

WEDNESDAY

Key Swim Anaerobic Threshold session

Warm-up:	3 x	2 x 100 freestyle on 10 seconds rest
		4 x 50 stroke or kick on 10 seconds rest
	4 x 100 m freestyle as:	25 drill
		75 swim *on 15 seconds rest*
Main set:	1 x 400	
	1 x 300	
	2 x 200	
	4 x 50 *all with 10-30 seconds rest at 85% effort (HR#3)*	
Cool-down:	4 x 75 pull easy on 10 seconds rest	
	6 x 50 choice on 10 seconds rest	

Bike 60-90 minutes easy ride at HR#1

THURSDAY

Key Run Intervals	
Warm-up:	20 minutes gradual warm-up and stretch
	8 x accelerations on grass, trail or road
Main set:	4-5 x 1000m on soft hilly surface if available
	or on the track or road, on a 5-7 minutes interval
	1-1:30 minutes easy jog between each
	Run odd ones at even 10km pace (HR#3-mid to high), even ones start at 1/2 marathon pace and finish at 5km pace (HR#2-high to #4-low)- keep moving between intervals.
	2 x 20-50 drills of each
	12-14 x accelerations
	Do these only if you have not done them Tuesday or plan to do on Friday.
Cool-down:	20 minutes easy and stretch

Weights 2 x 15 medium to heavy. **Endurance Phase**

FRIDAY

This day is optional. If you're tired or time strapped, take it off.

Swim Sprint session		
Warm-up:	16 x 50 as:	3 freestyle
		1 kick *on 10 seconds rest*
	200 drill (your choice)	
	200 kick	
Main set:	6-8 x 100 as: 1 fast/1 easy *on 45 seconds rest*	
	You can't go fast unless you take the full rest, and it's about going FAST today!	
Cool-down:	300 easy pull	

Bike 60 minute easy ride at HR#1

Run 30-50 minutes at HR#1 with drills and accelerations at end

SATURDAY

Swim Optional easy 30 minute swim of your choice

Key Bike 210-270 minute long ride at HR#1-2

It's very important to keep this ride aerobic. We'll be riding this harder when we're at the right point in the program.

Key Run 20-30 minute T-run at HR#1-2

SUNDAY

Bike Optional 60-90 minute easy ride at HR#1

Key Run 90-105 minutes

Emphasis on Sunday's run is still building a long aerobic run at HR#1-2. Still important to keep this run aerobic/comfortable.

Weights Same as Thursday

WEEK #11: BUILD

MONDAY

Swim Technique session		
Warm-up:	2 x	300 freestyle
		200 kick
		100 choice *all easy on 20 seconds rest*
Main set:	5 x 200 pull or swim easy to moderate with perfect form on 15 seconds rest	
	2 x	400 freestyle pull or swim
		(whichever you did not do on the last set)
		on 30 seconds rest between each
Cool-down:	12 x 50 choice easy with 10 seconds rest after each	

TUESDAY

Key Bike 70 minute turbo workout **Climb-O-Rama**	
Warm-up:	15-20 minutes gradual warm-up
Main set:	2 x 6 minutes, building 1 gear harder
	every minute, HR#3-low as a maximum
	2 minutes easy spin between each
	2 x 4/3 minutes big gear
	1 minute normal cadence after each
	at 80-100RPM
	HR#3-low to mid as a max, alternate one seated/one standing. That means that you alternate 4 minutes standing/3 minutes seated and then 4 minutes seated/3 minutes standing.
	10 minutes steady at HR#3-low as: 1 minute fast spin at 100RPM or greater
	1 minute standing Big Gear
	1 minute seated Big Gear
	1 x 15 seconds fast spinning jumps
	1:45 easy spin after each
	3 x 15 seconds Big Gear jumps
	1:45 easy spin after each
Cool-down:	10-15 minutes gradual cool-down

Key Run 20-30 minute T-run at HR#1-2

WEDNESDAY

Key Swim Anaerobic session

Warm-up:	3 x 300 as:	1 freestyle
		1 kick
		1 freestyle *all on 30 seconds rest*
	4 x 100 as:	1 freestyle drill
		1 stroke *on 20 seconds rest*
Main set:	20 x 100 as:	8 on 15 seconds rest at 85% hard, HR#3-mid
		8 on 10 seconds rest at 90% very hard, HR#3-high
		4 on 5 seconds rest at 95% very, very hard, HR#4
Cool-down:	4 x 50 pull easy on 10 seconds rest	
	200 choice	

Bike Easy 60-90 minutes at HR#1-2

THURSDAY

Key Run Track

Warm-up:	15-20 minutes easy to moderate
	6 acceleration runs
Main set:	3 mile SUB THRESHOLD steady time trial
	Keep this at 10-15 beats below AT, HR#3-low to mid, or just starting to hit a somewhat hard effort. This should NOT be anywhere near maximum effort or 10km pace. More like half marathon pace. Think control.
	6 more accelerations
Cool-down:	15-20 minutes easy to moderate

Weights 2 x 15 reps light to medium

Same as it ever was... Only increase weight in the exercises where your last 2 to 3 repetitions of each set are feeling easy (like you could still do 3 more after #15).

FRIDAY

(Again, this is an optional day of training.)

Swim Sprint session	
Warm-up:	50 kick
	50 freestyle on 15 seconds rest
Main set:	2 x 100 freestyle easy on 30 seconds rest
	2 x 50 IM fast on 20 seconds rest
	4 x 25 freestyle fast on 30 seconds rest
Cool-down:	300 pull easy
Bike 60 minute easy ride at HR#1	
Run 30-50 minutes at HR#1 with drills and accelerations at end	

SATURDAY

Swim Optional easy 30 minute swim of your choice
Key Bike 240-300 minute long ride at HR#1-2
Key Run 20-30 minute T-run at HR#1-2

SUNDAY

Bike Optional 60-90 minute easy ride at HR#1
If you're overworked, forget this one. Ride the couch instead.
Key Run 100-120 minute long run at HR#1-2
Weights Same as Thursday

WEEK #12: RECOVERY

MONDAY

Swim Technique session

Warm-up:	200 freestyle	
	200 choice	
	200 kick	
	200 choice *all easy on 20 seconds rest*	
Main set:	6 x 150 as:	50 freestyle
		50 stroke
		50 freestyle *all on 15 seconds rest*
	4 x 300 freestyle easy to moderate with 30 seconds between each	
	Focus on stroke count and smooth swimming	
Cool-down:	5 x 100 easy choice with 15 rest between each	

TUESDAY

Key Bike Turbo session Roller Coaster Workout

Warm-up:	15-20 minutes of easy to moderate riding	
	3 x 1 minutes fast spin	
	30 seconds easy	
Main set:	18 minutes Roller Coaster continuous as:	1 minute Big Gear seated at HR#2
		1 minute fast spin at HR#2
		1 minute faster spin at HR#3
	3 x 1 minute fast spin	
	30 seconds easy	
	Make the fast spins progressive. In other words, do each minute of work as follows: 20 seconds faster than normal cadence (100-110RPM), the second 20 seconds faster yet (120-130RPM), and the final 20 seconds as fast as you can maintain while staying seated and smooth. Focus on even pressure against the pedal all the way around the pedal stroke!	

	12 minutes Roller Coaster as:	1 minute Big Gear standing at HR#2
		1 minute fast spin at HR#2
		1 minute faster spin at HR#3
Cool-down:	10-15 minutes gradual cool-down	

Key Run 15-20 minute T-run at HR#1-2, performed within 10 minutes of finishing the turbo workout

WEDNESDAY

Key Swim Aerobic session

Warm-up:	4 x 200 as:	1 freestyle
		1 kick
		1 pull
		1 choice
Main set:	7 x 300 steady at HR#2 high with 30 seconds rest	
	Swim the first 4, then pull the last 3 – you're starting to see what the reality of Ironman swimming will be like.	
Cool-down:	8 x 75 as:	3 freestyle
		2 kick
		2 drill
		1 choice *all on 15 seconds rest easy*

THURSDAY

Key Run Moderate run	
Warm-up:	15 minutes warm-up and stretch
Main set:	20-30 minutes moderate run
	with 6 x 1 minute pick-ups at HR#3
	with 3-4 minutes easy between.
	Not wide out sprints, but a "feel-good" tempo pace.
	2 x 20-50 drills of each
	12-14 x accelerations
	Do these only if you have not done them on Tuesday
Cool-down:	10 minutes gradual cool-down and stretch

Weights 2 x 15 reps of each exercise medium to heavy

FRIDAY

Off

SATURDAY

Swim Optional easy 30 minute swim of your choice

Key Bike 120-180 minute long ride at HR#1

Key Run 20 minute T-run at HR#1-2

SUNDAY

Bike Optional 60 minute easy ride at HR#1

Key Run 60-80 minute long run at HR#1-2

Weights Same as Thursday

QUESTIONS & ANSWERS

Q: I live in Canada and it's too cold to bike outside, so I do all my rides on my turbo-trainer. Is this cool?

A: If you're stuck indoors on a stationary trainer for all rides, make sure you're doing 50-75% (max) of the prescribed time in the schedule. For example, if the long ride says "4 hours" and you have to do this on a stationary trainer, you should go 2 to 3 hours. We don't want anyone going mental.

Q: I've been feeling pretty strong on my long runs and rides. Is it okay to crank it up a notch in intensity?

A: It's still early in your march to the Ironman. If you want to show up at the starting line on race day rested and ready to go, save the super long and hard workouts for later. Trust us, they're coming. Better to hit the race starting line 10-20% undertrained than 1% overtrained. CONSISTENCY is the key. Find what fits into your weekly schedule, taking into account family life and work, and stay consistent.

Q. I'm a little overwhelmed by all the race wheels on the market. What kind of wheels do I pick for speed?

A. How do you choose? Mark Allen was notorious for taking a wide selection of wheels to the San Diego Velodrome and timing himself over 3000 meters at a set heart rate with each combination. Using this method, he could choose his wheel set-up with full confidence that it was the fastest possible. Sometimes he rode a tri or quad spoke on the rear with a deep section wheel on the front, and sometimes he rode with deep section wheels on both front and rear.
You may not have the luxury of a brother in the bike-shop business, so start by asking yourself what you can afford and then ask around for opinions. Talk to other athletes who have made the plunge and speak to the staff at different bike shops. Weigh up all of this information for yourself and make your choice. Every wheel manufacturer will tell you why their product is superior to all others. In the end, it's your job to sort through all the claims and wind tunnel tests and come up with what works best for you.

As far as tires go, sew-ups or tubulars are a lot easier to change in a race situation than clinchers. While you used to be able to get more pressure (and, hence lower the rolling resistance of your wheel) into a sew-up tire (still the case with some brands), there are some high pressure clinchers out there that are quite fast (Vredestein, for example). However, I still favor sew-up tires for races due to the speed with which you can change them. Since sew-ups are expensive, a common strategy is to train on clinchers and race on sew-ups.

Don't forget to make sure whatever you get looks good on your bike — after all, it's not how fast you go, it's how good you look.

A stationary trainer will prepare you physically for the bike portion of the race, but regular group rides will prepare you to handle the dynamics of passing, being passed and riding in a pack.

CHAPTER 7
Ironman-Specific Base
Weeks 13-18

This is the third six-week program and the time is drawing near for the "real" training to begin. The emphasis over the next six weeks will go from the gym to your actual Ironman-specific training (if you haven't done it already, it's time to warn your family, friends and co-workers that you're about to enter the final nine weeks of preparation in the middle of this training phase).

WEIGHT TRAINING

Depending on your background in the gym, you'll either enter the power phase or remain in the endurance phase for another four weeks. If the past 12 weeks is the first time you've had a consistent strength-training program in a year or more, you will remain in the endurance phase. If, however, you were on a consistent strength-training program prior to beginning this program, you'll go into the power phase.

If you're entering the power phase in the gym, make sure you review the characteristics of this phase in the Weight Training Chapter. You only "power" large muscle group exercises and must make sure you're well warmed up, as you'll be using heavier weights. We strongly suggest that you do NOT go to failure (but get close) and that you have a spotter for "powered" exercises. The same basic rules of lifting apply in the power phase (speed of execution, full range of motion, and breathing).

In the last two weeks of this six-week increment, EVERYONE will enter the "chisel phase." At this point, you will need to review the characteristics of this phase — no legs, increased speed of execution and lighter weights. You should be getting excited because, only a week after entering the "chisel" phase, you'll begin to feel much better in your sport-specific (swim, bike, and run) workouts. This comes at exactly the right time, as your Ironman-specific training takes precedence.

A CHANGE IN FOCUS

The second three weeks of this six-week training period marks the beginning of your specific Ironman preparation. The critical workouts become the long rides and runs. Make sure you're taking advantage of the opportunity to practice your pacing, nutrition and hydration strategies in these sessions to find out what works and doesn't work.

We can't emphasize this enough — group workouts are fine, but don't turn them into races. Especially on the Saturday long rides and Sunday long runs. Don't go too hard — these are meant to be performed at a relatively EASY intensity. When we get to the final six weeks, you can begin to do the long runs and rides at what you expect to be realistic race pace.

Transition runs (as important as ever) will begin to increase in length a little. Remember, the point of these is to become more efficient at getting your running legs under you after the bike — NOT intensity or distance (you have specific days for that).

You should be doing your running drills and accelerations on a consistent basis. Don't forego these because you think they don't apply to Ironman – they do! Again, these have been scheduled at the end of your track/intensity run workouts but are best done at the end of one of your easier runs (when your legs aren't fatigued from a hard workout but are warmed up). If you know you won't do them in an unstructured environment (easy run days), however, go ahead and do them at the end of your key run day (the intensity/track workout). If you are becoming fatigued towards the end of this six-week period, realize that the first week of the final six-week period (next schedule) is a recovery week. It's okay to get into a fatigued state, as long as it doesn't last longer then four days. If you're still tired after four days, simply decrease the intensity of the harder swim, bike and run during the week so you have enough energy for the longer weekend workouts and avoid injury or illness.

WEEK #13: BUILD

MONDAY

Swim Aerobic session		
Warm-up:	12 x 75 as:	6 freestyle
		6 drill *on 15 seconds rest*
	8 x 25 as:	25 IM order
		25 freestyle *on 10 seconds rest*
Main set:	600 freestyle pull easy on 20 seconds rest	
	2 x 300 freestyle easy to moderate on 20 sec rest	
	3 x 200 freestyle easy to moderate on 15 sec rest	
	400 pull easy	
Cool-down:	8 x 25 as:	one drill
		1 choice easy

TUESDAY

Key Bike 75 minute turbo workout **Anaerobic Threshold (AT) Intervals**	
Warm-up:	15-20 minutes
	3 x 30 seconds SLD
	30 seconds both legs
Main set:	5 minutes steady in aero-bars at 90-100 cadence
	1 minute Big Gear
	1 minute fast spin
	1 minute recovery
	4 minute steady in aero-bars at 90-100 cadence
	then 1 minute Big Gear
	then 1 minute fast spin
	then 1 minute recovery.
	3 x 40 seconds SLD
	20 seconds both legs
	3 minutes steady in aero-bars at 90-100 cadence
	then 1 minute Big Gear
	then 1 minute fast spin
	then 1 minute recovery
	2 minutes steady in aero-bars at 90-100 cadence
	then 1 minute Big Gear
	then 1 minute fast spin
	then 1 minute recovery
	All at HR#3-low to -mid and using aero-bars
	10 minute steady at HR#2-3
	choice of gear, cadence and position
Cool-down:	10-15 minutes

Key Run T-run of 25-35 minutes run performed after your bike intervals (within 10 min) at a easy to moderate effort of HR#1-2.

Keep the intensity of this T-run down, as next week's T-run will be a little harder – closer to Ironman marathon race pace.

WEDNESDAY

Key Swim Anaerobic Threshold session		
Warm-up:	3 x 300 as:	1 freestyle
		1 kick
		1 IM *all on 30 seconds rest*
Main set:	2 x 400 freestyle on 20 seconds rest 200 kick	
	3 x 200 freestyle on 15 seconds rest 200 kick	
	5 x 100 freestyle on 10 seconds rest *all at 85% (HR#3)*	
Cool-down:	8 x 50 as:	1 drill
		1 easy
		1 fast
		1 easy choice *all on 15 seconds rest*
Bike Optional 60-90 minute easy ride at HR#1-2		

THURSDAY

Key Run Intervals	
Warm-up:	20 minutes and stretch
	4-8 x accelerations
Main set:	1 x 5 minutes
	4 x 2 minutes
	1 x 5 minutes
	All steady at HR#3-low to medium with 2 minutes moderate (HR#2-low) between each. Not killer intervals, but you're starting to get up to some good speed. Depending upon how you feel running, perform these intervals on varying terrain or the track. Varying terrain will force you to pace yourself without the luxury of knowing where you are. If you need to learn to equate pace with perceived effort, the track might be the call.
	2 x 40 reps of all drills
Cool-down:	15-20 minutes and stretch
Weights 30-60 minute Power Phase workout	

FRIDAY

Swim Sprint session

Warm-up:	600 freestyle	
	400 kick	
	200 stroke	
	8 x 100 as:	25 drill
		25 stroke
		50 freestyle *all on 15 seconds rest*
Main set:	8 x 50 fast on 1 minute rest	
Cool-down:	600 easy choice	

Bike Easy 60 minutes at HR#1

Only do this ride if you can do it easy — which means you'll finish the ride feeling like you didn't do anything.

Run 30-50 minutes easy, HR#1, with drills and accelerations at the end

As with the bike ride on this day, only perform it if you can do it easy and feel recovered afterwards.

SATURDAY

Swim Optional easy 30-45 minute swim of your choice

This is best done before the long bike ride or later in the day after the bike and run. Mix it up and make sure you do a swim before your long ride at least a couple of times during this six-week period to ensure you realize the nutritional and energetic implications of a decent swim before a long ride – just like you'll be facing in about 12 weeks.

Key Bike 180-240 minutes (3 to 4 hours)

Still just a long ride day. This week, we keep it a little shorter, as you will have a longer T-run and a longer Sunday run.

Run 30-40 minute T-run at HR#1-2

Perform this after your long bike ride (within 10 minutes) at an easy to moderate effort of HR#1-2. The purpose of this run is to see if your nutrition and hydration on the long ride was adequate. If not, the transition run should tell the story.

SUNDAY

Bike Easy 60-90 minute ride at HR#1

If you can't do this ride easy, then don't do it. With the longer long run, you might be better off doing 1 to 1.5 hours on the couch! Do what enhances recovery.

Key Run 100-120 minute long run at HR#1-2

Weights Same as Thursday

WEEK #14: BUILD

MONDAY

Swim Aerobic session

Warm-up:	4 x 250 as:	2 freestyle
		1 kick
		1 drill *all on 30 seconds rest*
Main set:	6 x 400 freestyle steady at HR#2 low (moderate) on 30 seconds rest *Swim #1, 2, 5, 6 and pull 3 and 4*	
Cool-down:	200 choice	

TUESDAY

Key Bike 70-minute Turbo AT Intervals

Warm up:	6 x 40 seconds fast spin
	20 seconds easy
	Build each one faster than the previous one so you're fully warmed up before the main set.
Main set:	10/8/6/4 minutes
	All steady at HR#3-mid to high, 3 minutes recovery between each. Try to stay in aero-bars as much as possible and keep your cadence between 90-100 rpm.
	4 x 30 seconds very fast spin
	1 minute easy
Cool-down:	10-15 minutes

Key Run A 25-35 minute run performed after your bike intervals (within 10 minutes) at a harder effort of HR#2-3.

Not hammering, but just a good steady pace.

WEDNESDAY

Key Swim Anaerobic Threshold session		
Warm-up:	4 x 150 as:	100 freestyle
		50 stroke *all on 15 seconds rest*
Main set:	6 x 400 as:	5 x 400 on 30 seconds rest
		4 x 100 on 10 seconds rest
		all at 85%
Cool-down:	5 x 100 easy as:	2 kick
		1 drill
		2 choice *all on 15 seconds rest*

Bike Optional 60-90 minute easy ride at HR#1-2.

If you're tired or pressed for time by the middle of this second build week, consider shortening or even skipping this ride.

THURSDAY

Key Run Intervals	
Warm-up:	20 minutes and stretch
	followed by 6-10 accelerations
Main set:	6 x 5 minutes steady at HR#3-low to mid
	2 minutes moderate between each
	As with last week, perform the intervals on varying terrain or track (switch it up, making it different every week). Become very familiar with pace versus perceived effort and HR, so you can recognize what is realistic on race day.
	2 x 40 drills of each
Cool-down:	15-20 minutes and stretch

Weights 30-60 minutes, Power or Endurance.

FRIDAY

Optional. Take the day off if you're tired, or only do one workout.

Swim Sprint session		
Warm-up:	800 choice	
	8 x 50 IM order on 15 seconds rest	
Main set:	12 x 100 descend 1-4 (#4 very fast)	
	all on 30 seconds rest	
Cool-down:	6 x 100 easy as:	50 freestyle drill
		50 choice *all on 15 seconds rest*
Bike Easy 60-90 minutes at HR#1		
Run Easy 30-50 minutes at HR#1		

SATURDAY

Swim Optional easy 30-45 minutes
Key Bike 4-5 hour ride at HR#2
Key Run 35-45 minute transition run at HR#1
No one will feel good for the first 5 to 10 minutes but, if you've paid attention to your nutritional and hydration needs on the long ride, you might be surprised at how good you feel for the latter two-thirds to three-quarters of this run.

SUNDAY

Bike Optional 60-90 minute ride at HR#1
If you can't do this ride easy, then don't do it. Perform your long run first and then ride later if you have time and energy.
Key Run 90-105 minutes at HR#1-2
Shorter run this week than last. Keep it aerobic and comfortable. You'll be on tired legs, so don't force it.
Weights Same as Thursday

WEEK #15: RECOVERY

MONDAY

Swim Aerobic session		
Warm-up:	10 x 25 freestyle on 5 seconds rest	
	8 x 50 choice on 10 seconds rest	
	5 x 100 as:	50 freestyle
		50 choice *all on 15 seconds rest*
Main set:	50-150-250-350-450-350-250-150-50	
	All easy freestyle on 20-30 seconds rest	
Cool-down:	12 x 25 as:	1 fast
		3 easy choice *on 10 seconds rest*

TUESDAY

Key Bike 70-minute turbo-trainer workout		
Warm-up:	15 minutes	
	4 x 1 minute fast spin	
	1 minute easy	
Main set:	3 x 2 minutes	
	Descend from HR#2-3-high with cadence 90-100	
	2 minutes easy between each	
	2 x 30 seconds SLD	
	30 seconds both legs	
	12 minute Roller Coaster as:	1 minute big gear (HR#2)
		1 minute fast spin (HR#2)
		1 minute fast (HR#3)
	3 x 2 minutes descend from HR#3-#4-plus at your choice of cadence	
	3 minutes easy between each	
Cool-down:	10-15 minutes easy	
Key Run A shorter transition run this recovery week of 15-20 minutes performed after your bike intervals (within 10 minutes) at an easy effort of HR#1		

WEDNESDAY

Key Swim Aerobic session

Warm-up:	2 x	
	6 x 50 freestyle on 10 seconds rest	
	300 choice on 30 seconds rest	
	12 x 50 as:	3 back
		1 freestyle *all on 10 seconds rest*
Main set:	30 x 50 as:	5 on 10 seconds rest
	3 x	5 on 5 seconds rest
	All easy to moderate aerobic.	
Cool-down:	200 choice	

Bike Optional easy ride of 60 minutes at HR#1

THURSDAY

Key Run Fartlek

Similar to the last Recovery week.

Warm-up:	20 minutes and stretch.
	8-12 accelerations
	Walk back so that you are fully recovered after each.
Main set:	20-30 minutes of fartlek
	Running how you feel and what intervals you feel like doing while keeping within HR#1-#3-low.
	2 x 40 drills of each
Cool-down:	10 minutes and stretch.

Weights 30-60 minutes, Power or Endurance

FRIDAY

Off

SATURDAY

Swim Optional easy 30 minute swim of your choice

Key Bike 120-180 minutes at HR#1

Enjoy it, as the key Ironman training will start next week.

Key Run 15-20 minute T-run at HR#1-2

SUNDAY

Bike Optional easy 60-minute ride at HR#1

Key Run 60-80 minute long run at HR#1

We're bringing the long run down in duration to honor Recovery Week.

Weights 30-60 minutes of Power or Endurance

WEEK #16: IM BASE

MONDAY

Swim Aerobic session

Warm-up:	4 x 200 as:	2 freestyle
		1 kick
		1 drill *all on 20 seconds rest*
Main set:	5 x 500 freestyle easy pace on 45 seconds rest	
	Swim #1, 2, and 5, option to pull 3 and 4	
Cool-down:	200 choice	

TUESDAY

Key Bike Turbo **AT Intervals**

Warm-up:	15-20 minutes
	3 x 40 seconds SLD
	20 seconds both legs
Main set:	6 minutes steady in aero-bars at 90-100 cadence
	1 minute Big Gear
	1 minute fast spin
	1 minute recovery
	5 minutes steady in aero-bars at 90-100 cadence
	1 minute Big Gear
	1 minute fast spin
	1 minute recovery
	2 x 50 seconds SLD
	10 seconds both legs
	4 minute steady in aero-bars at 90-100 cadence
	1 minute Big Gear
	1 minute fast spin
	1 minute recovery
	3 minutes steady in aero-bars at 90-100 cadence
	1 minute big gear

	then 1 minute fast spin
	then 1 minute recovery
	All at HR#3-low to mid and in aero-bars
	10 minutes
	Switch gear, cadence, speed or position every 30 seconds, keeping heart rate anywhere above HR#2.
Cool-down:	10-15 minutes

Key Run 15-20 minute transition run at HR#1-2

WEDNESDAY

Key Swim Anaerobic Threshold session

Warm-up:	800 easy to moderate choice	
Main set:	4-5 x 500 as:	1-500 straight with 30 seconds rest
		1-5 x 100 on 5 seconds rest
	All at race pace or HR#3 medium or at a somewhat hard to hard effort.	
Cool-down:	800 continuous as:	50 drill
		50 stroke
		100 freestyle

Bike 60-90 minutes easy ride at HR#1

You're doing this only if time and energy is available. This week it shouldn't be a problem, as you're coming off a Recovery week —right? If you're still tired, though, it's still better to skip it and make sure your long ride and run on the weekend are optimal!

THURSDAY

Key Run Tempo

Warm-up:	20 minutes and stretch
	followed by 6-10 accelerations
Main set:	30-40 minutes steady at HR#2 high to HR#3 low
	Try to hit the hilly trails or rolling roads and learn to maintain effort conserving on the ups and coming off the top of each hill and using the downhill to your advantage.
Cool-down:	20 minutes and stretch

Weights 60-90 minutes. *Final week of Endurance or Power.*

FRIDAY

(Optional day off)

Swim Sprint session

Warm-up:	1000 easy freestyle	
	12 x 50 as:	1 kick
		1 drill *both on 10 seconds rest*
		300 easy pull
Main set:	10 x 100 as:	1 fast
		1 easy *both on 1-2 minutes rest*
Cool-down:	4 x 100 as:	50 drill
		50 choice *all*
		on 15 seconds rest

Bike 60 minute easy ride at HR#1

Remember that the weekend rides are now KEY, so don't do this ride if you're already toast — you'll need energy for tomorrow.

Run 30-50 minutes at HR#1 with drills and accelerations at end

SATURDAY

Swim Optional easy 30-minute swim of your choice

Key Bike 270-330 minute long ride at HR#1-2

Key Run A 40-50 minute run performed after your long bike ride (within 10 minutes) at an easy to moderate effort of HR#1-2

It's starting to get longer. Again, one of the primary reasons for this run is to perfect your pacing, nutritional, and hydration strategy on the bike. If you didn't do it right, it will be readily apparent during this run.

SUNDAY

Key Bike Optional 60-minute easy ride at HR#1

Optional, but this is also a day when you can get some additional cycling miles into your legs — as long as it's after the long run. Keep it in the small ring (easy gearing!).

Key Run 105-120 minutes this weekend at HR#1-2

Keep it under control and try to mimic the pace you hope to handle on race day.

Weights 60-90 minutes. Final week of Endurance or Power.

WEEK #17: BUILD

MONDAY

Swim Aerobic session	
Warm-up:	10 x 100 freestyle easy on 10 seconds rest
	6 x 75 kick on 10 seconds rest
Main set:	2 x
	6 x 50 freestyle on 10 seconds rest
	3 x 100 pull on 20 seconds rest
	300 choice on 1 minutes rest
	all easy aerobic
Cool-down:	200 choice

TUESDAY

Key Bike 70 minute turbo	
Warm-up:	15-20 minutes easy
	6 x 50 seconds fast spin
	1:10 easy
Main set:	12/10/8 minutes all steady at HR#3-mid
	3 minutes recovery after each, try to stay down in the aero position and keep your rpm constant at 85-95RPM.
	4 x 20 seconds very fast spin
	1:40 easy
Cool-down:	15-20 minutes
Key Run 30-40 minute T-run	
Add in drills and accelerations towards the end of the run if you have time.	

WEDNESDAY

Key Swim Anaerobic session	
Warm-up:	800 choice
Main set:	3 x
	300 fast (HR#4) on 45 seconds rest
	then 4-6x 100 on 10 seconds rest at HR#2-3
	take 1 minute extra rest between sets
Cool-down:	800 choice easy

Bike Optional 60-90 minute easy ride at HR#1

How are you feeling? If you're extremely tired, skip this ride. Still doing well and want to boost your cycling volume? Do it.

THURSDAY

Key Run Intervals	
Warm-up:	20 minutes and stretch
	5-6 x accelerations
Main set:	2 x 5 minutes steady at HR#3-low
	2 minutes moderate between
	10 minutes steady at HR#3-mid
	with 4 minutes moderate recovery after
	5 x 3 minutes steady at HR#3-mid to high
	with 2 minutes easy between each
	This is best performed off road.
	2 x 40 reps of all drills
Cool-down:	15-20 minutes and stretch

Weights 30-60 minutes, 2 x 10-12 light to medium Chisel.

All workouts are optional

Swim Sprint session		
Warm-up:	400 freestyle	
	300 kick	
	200 stroke	
	100 drill	
	4 x 100 as:	50 stroke
		50 freestyle *both on 15 seconds rest*
Main set:	16 x 50 as:	1 fast
		2 easy *both on 20 seconds rest*
		400 pull easy
		1 minute rest
		200 freestyle fast
Cool-down:	200 choice	

Bike 60 minute easy ride at HR#1
You have a big ride on Saturday, so don't blow it here. Ride for recovery only, if at all.

Run 30-50 minutes at HR#1 with drills and accelerations at end.

SATURDAY

Swim Optional easy 30-minute swim of your choice

Remember to try to stack up at least one weekend day where you swim, ride long, then perform a T-run.

Key Bike 330-390 minutes (that's 5.5 to 6.5 hours!) at HR#1-2

Remember that this is your key ride, so get rested on Friday. Practice your race day nutrition and hydration.

Key Run 50-60 minute T-run at HR#1-2

Weights Same as Thursday

SUNDAY

Bike Optional 60-minute easy ride at HR#1

Based on the length of yesterday's ride, you might be better off staying out of the saddle today.

Key Run 120-150 minutes (2 to 2.5 hours!) at HR#1-2

Get the time on your legs but keep it aerobic!

Weights Same as Thursday

© iStockphoto/Thinkstock

WEEK #18: RECOVERY

MONDAY

Swim Aerobic session

Warm-up:	6 x 250 as:	1, 3 and 5 freestyle
		2,4, 6-100 freestyle
		100 stroke
		50 kick, *all on 30 seconds rest*
Main set:	4 x 200 easy as:	1 kick
		1 IM
		1 drill
		1 freestyle *on 20 seconds rest*
	5 x 100 as:	25 fast
		75 easy *on 15 seconds rest*
	12 x 50 stroke on 10 seconds rest	
Cool-down:	4 x 200 easy pull on 20 seconds rest	

TUESDAY

Key Bike Turbo AT Intervals

Warm-up:	15-20 minutes easy
	3 x 1 minute SLD
	1 minute both legs
Main set:	7 minutes steady in aero-bars at 90-100 cadence
	1 minute Big Gear standing at ‹70 rpm
	1 minute fast spin
	1 minute recovery
	6 minutes steady in aero-bars at 90-100 cadence
	1 minute Big Gear standing
	1 minute fast spin
	1 minute recovery
	45 seconds SLD
	1:15 both legs
	5 minutes steady in aero-bars at 90-100 cadence
	1 minute Big Gear standing
	1 minute fast spin
	1 minute recovery
	4 minutes steady in aero-bars at 90-100 cadence
	1 minute Big Gear standing
	1 minute fast spin
	1 minute recovery
	All at HR#3 mid to high and in aero-bars
	10 minute ride
	Switch gear, cadence, speed or position every 30 seconds, keeping heart rate anywhere above HR#2.
Cool-down:	10-15 minute

Key Run 30-40 minute T-run, easy to moderate effort of HR#1-2

WEDNESDAY

Key Swim Anaerobic session

Warm-up:	800 choice	
Main set:	5-6 x 500 as:	500 straight
		5 x 100 on 10 seconds rest
	All at race pace or slightly faster, HR#3-mid or at a somewhat hard to hard effort.	
Cool-down:	400-800 choice easy	

THURSDAY

Key Run Tempo

Warm-up:	20 minutes and stretch
	5-6 x accelerations
Main set:	35-45 minutes steady at HR#2-3
	on varying terrain
	2 x 40 reps of all drills
Cool-down:	15-20 minutes easy and stretch.

Weights 30-60 minutes, 2 x 10-12 light to medium. *Chisel*

FRIDAY

(All workouts optional)

Swim Sprint session

Warm-up:	12 x 50 as:	2 freestyle
		1 stroke
		1 kick *on 10 seconds rest*
	12 x 25 descending 1-4 on 10 seconds rest	
Main set:	8 x 100 as:	1 fast
		1 easy *on 30 seconds rest*
Cool-down:	200 choice	

SATURDAY

Swim Optional easy 30-minute swim of your choice

Key Bike 300-360 minutes (5 to 6 hours) at HR#1-2

Slightly shorter this week, but you will have your longest run on Sunday.

Key Run 20 minute T-run at HR#1-2

A little shorter this week, as you have your longest run on Sunday

SUNDAY

Bike Optional 45-60 minute easy ride at HR#1

Today you're doing your longest long run, so it's probably best to skip any easy riding. If, however, you feel it will enhance your recovery from the run to spin easy for 45 to 60 minutes, go ahead and do so.

Key Run 150-180 minute long run at HR#1-2

Weights Same as Thursday

QUESTIONS & ANSWERS

Q: Is this a point where I should really try and push the intensity of my swimming?

A: There's plenty of quality swimming written into the schedule, but don't sacrifice technique for speed. Remember, the Ironman swim is not about how fast you get out of the water, but about racing the swim while burning as little energy as possible. Technique and efficiency — that's what your swim training is really all about.

Q. How should I deal with missing out on training due to a cold or injury?

A. If you miss one to three days of the program, ease back into the program for one to two days. Don't go hard for the first two days after a layoff. If you miss a full week due to health, family, work, or bass fishing tournaments, give yourself 3-5 days to ease back into the program. Use common sense — longer and harder is not always the best policy.

Don't do all your swim training in the pool. Open water swimming and swimming in "traffic" involve some very specific skills.

CHAPTER 8
Race Phase
Weeks 19-24

This is it – the last six weeks prior to the big day! The first of these weeks is focused on recovery (from the last three "base" weeks). When in doubt, go easier or not at all – the goal is to absorb the training you've done to this point and be ready for the next two weeks of Ironman-specific work. The second and third weeks are "hard" Ironman-specific weeks, followed by a very gradual three-week taper.

WEIGHT TRAINING

In the first two weeks of this phase, EVERYONE is in the "chisel phase." For the final four weeks of this program, you won't do any weight training. That's right, you don't have to lift weights any more.

TRAINING NOTES

By now, you should be familiar with the number of calories per hour you can absorb while riding and running. Make sure you're practicing your eating and drinking during your long training sessions. Take note of what, how much and when you eat the evening before these long workouts in order to plan better for your meal the night before the race.

If you don't know the following, you haven't been paying attention:
- It's okay to move workouts around to suit your life/local training schedule. If you have a group long run on Saturday and like to ride on Sunday, switch these two days in the program.

- One simple rule: while it's okay to put a swim workout on the same day as a bike or run, try NOT to have a long/hard bike on the same day as a long/hard run. We keep repeating this because, yes, it's that important.

- Especially during the recovery week and the taper, you need to pay close attention to your training/overtraining status. You may need to do even less than what we've recommended. Remember to keep the focus on recovering and absorbing all of the work you've done during these weeks.

When performing your long workouts in weeks 2, 3, 4 and 5 of this period, you can bring the intensity up to realistic race pace (what you expect to be able to maintain on race day) or slightly faster.

A good taper will make your race. Refusing to perform a taper will jeopardize it. During the taper, your focus is on RECOVERY! When in doubt, either shorten or go easier on a given workout … or eliminate it altogether! The point is to keep things moving while getting rested. Remember that fatigue usually trails training by two to five days. If, when you first back off, you feel worse (more tired), don't panic! Go with it and keep things at a very low intensity — and cut the duration of your workouts. Better yet, when faced with this situation, take an additional day or two OFF!

If you're racing on one of these weekends, no problem. We strongly suggest that you get in at least one race before Ironman race day. Just substitute your race for Sunday's workouts and then add on a 20-40-minute run after the race as a cool-down. Perform your Saturday workout as usual, but reduce the length of the T-run to 15-20 minutes and very easy. The only caution is during the following week's workouts. If you're not recovered from the race, make sure you take it easy on the harder Tuesday and/or Thursday sessions, so you are rested and ready for the longer weekend workouts.

There's nothing like the feeling of crossing that finish line...
no matter how often you do it, no matter what your final time.
You have just become part of an athletic elite.
Be proud!

WEEK #19: RECOVERY

MONDAY

Swim Aerobic session		
Warm-up:	10 x 100 as:	2 freestyle
		2 stroke
		1 kick *on 15 seconds rest*
Main set:	8-10 x 200 at 80% HR#2 low on 20 seconds rest	
Cool-down:	500 choice	

TUESDAY

Key Bike 75 minute turbo workout	
Warm-up:	15 minutes easy
	2 x 20 seconds fast spin
	40 seconds easy in between
Main set:	1/2/3/4/5/4/3/2/1 minutes
	Descend from HR#2 on first & second minutes, then HR#3-4 on the way down. 2 minutes easy between each. Keep the majority of the intervals in the aero bars at 85-95RPM.
	To make the session more interesting, try 30 seconds-1 minute in a Big Gear seated and standing anytime during the even intervals.
	2 x 30 second SLD
	30 seconds both legs
Cool-down:	15 minutes easy
Key Run 15-20 minute T-run at HR#1-2	

WEDNESDAY

Key Swim Aerobic session

Warm-up:	4 x 200 as:	1 freestyle
		1 back
		1 pull
	1 freestyle *all on 15 seconds rest*	
	16 x 25 as:	1 drill
	1 freestyle on 10 seconds rest	
Main set:	12 x 50 freestyle easy on 10 seconds rest	
	6 x 100 freestyle easy on 15 seconds rest	
	3 x 200 freestyle easy on 20 seconds rest	
Cool-down:	5 x 100 as:	50 kick
		50 choice *easy on 10 seconds rest*

Bike Optional 60-90 minute easy ride at HR#1-2

THURSDAY

Key Run Fartlek

Warm-up:	20 minutes and stretch. 3-6 accelerations
Main set:	20-40 minutes of fartlek running
	Run how you feel, at the intervals you feel like running. Just keep the heart-rate at HR#1-HR#3-low.
Cool-down:	15 minutes easy

Weights 30-60 minutes, 2x10 light to medium. *Chisel.*

FRIDAY

Off

SATURDAY

Swim Easy 30 minutes swim of your choice

Best performed before the long bike ride or later in the day after the bike and run.

Key Bike 2-3 hours week at HR#1

Shorter since this is a recovery week. Enjoy it, as the next three weeks are hard.

Key Run 30-40 minute T-run at HR#1-2

Perform this after your long bike ride (within 10 minutes) at an easy to moderate effort of HR #1-2. The purpose of this run is to see if your nutrition and hydration on the long ride was adequate. If not, the transition run should tell the story.

SUNDAY

Bike Optional 60-minute easy spin

Key Run 60-80 minute long run at HR#1-2

You'll need this shorter long run after the last two weekends.

Weights Same as Thursday

WEEK #20: HARD

MONDAY

Swim Aerobic session		
Warm-up:	16 x 50 as:	2 freestyle
		1 choice *on 10 seconds rest*
Main set:	21 x 100 steady pace at HR#2-high	
	(Somewhat Hard effort) on 15 seconds rest	
Cool-down:	3 x 200 as:	1 pull
		1 kick
		1 IM

TUESDAY

Key Bike 70-minute turbo Intervals	
Warm-up:	15-20 min
	3 x 30 seconds fast spin
	30 seconds easy
Main set:	4/8/12/8/4 minutes
	All steady at HR#3-low to -mid with 2 minutes recovery after each. Do most of the intervals in the aero bars keeping the cadence at 85-95RPM.
	If the butt and/or crotch go completely numb, stand up in a Big Gear for 30 seconds here or there.
	2 x 30 seconds fast spin/ 1:30 easy
Cool-down:	15-20 minutes easy
Key Run A 30-40 minute run T-run performed at HR#2	

WEDNESDAY

Key Swim Aerobic session	
Warm-up:	800 choice
Main set:	8 x 50 fast on 30 seconds rest
	6-7 x 300 on 30 seconds rest
	faster than race pace or HR#3
	(somewhat hard to hard effort)
	then 8 x 50 again even faster on 30 seconds rest
Cool-down:	800 choice

Bike Optional 60-90 minute easy ride at HR#1-2

THURSDAY

Key Run Intervals on the track, road or trails	
Warm-up:	20 minutes and stretch
	4-6 accelerations
Main set:	8 x 3 minutes steady at HR#3-mid to high
	2 minutes moderate recovery (HR#2)
Cool-down:	20-30 minutes easy to moderate

Weights Same as last week: Chisel phase workout

This is your final week of weight training!

FRIDAY

Swim Sprint session		
Warm-up:	1000 as:	175 freestyle
		25 stroke
		3 x 200 pull on 15 seconds rest
Main set:	12 x 75 alternating as:	1- 25 fast / 50 easy
		1-50 easy / 25 fast
		all on 30 seconds rest
Cool-down:	5 x 100 as:	2 kick
		2 drill
		1 choice *easy on 15 seconds rest*

SATURDAY

Swim Optional easy 30-45 minutes

Key Bike 360-420 minutes at HR#1-2

Yep, that's right: six to seven hours. The time refers to saddle time, not time spent away from home. Those 30 minute breaks at the 7-11 don't count as riding time.

Red alert: *Get your hydration and nutrition dialed during this ride.*

Key Run 40-50 minutes easy T-run performed after your long bike ride at an easy to moderate effort of HR #1-2

This one could hurt a bit after the very long ride, but take your time and tell yourself you don't need to hammer. This run will tell you if you've paid attention to your nutrition and hydration on the bike.

SUNDAY

Bike An easy 60-90 minutes ride at HR#1

If you can't do this ride easy, then best not to do it. Perform your long run first and then ride later if you have time and energy available.

Key Run 105-135 minutes at HR#1-2

Keep this run aerobic, moderate in length and intensity, as you had your longest ride the day before.

Weights Same as last week's workouts

After this, you can forget the weight room. Expect to feel some extra power in your regular training.

WEEK #21: HARD

MONDAY

Swim Aerobic session	
Warm-up:	500 freestyle
	500 pull
	500 choice *all easy on 1 minute rest*
Main set:	16 x 100 as:
	5 freestyle on 15 seconds rest
	5 x 50 kick/50 freestyle on 15 seconds rest
	5 freestyle again on 15 seconds rest
	all easy and aerobic
Cool-down:	400 choice

TUESDAY

Key Bike 70-minute turbo **Descending Intervals**	
Warm-up:	15-20 minutes easy
	4 x 15 seconds fast spin
	45 seconds easy
Main set:	15/12/10 minutes descending within each one
	from HR#2-high to HR #3-high
	4 minutes easy between each
	5 x 30 seconds fast spin
	1:30 easy between each
Cool-down:	15-20 minutes
Key Run 30-40 minutes T-run performed after your bike intervals (within 10 minutes) at HR#2.	
Not hammering, but just a good, up-beat pace.	

WEDNESDAY

Key Swim Aerobic session	
Warm-up:	800 choice
Main set:	6-8 x 400 at faster than race pace or HR#3 as:
	2-3 straight on 15 seconds rest
	2-3 broken into 4 x 100 on 5 seconds rest
	last 2-3 straight on 30 seconds rest
Cool-down:	600 easy choice
	It's not pretty, but it's a taste of reality when you're preparing for a 2.4 mile swim!
Bike Optional easy ride of 60 minutes at HR#1	

THURSDAY

Key Run Intervals on the track, road or trails	
Warm-up:	15-20 minutes
	4-6 x accelerations
Main set:	3 x 2 miles (or 15 minute intervals)
	At HR#3-low to -mid (about your pace for a 15km road race) with 400 meters (or 2-3 min) recovery
Cool-down:	20 minutes
Weights 30-60 minutes. Power or endurance.	

FRIDAY

All workouts are optional

Swim Sprint session

Warm-up:	800 freestyle easy	
	600 as:	50 drill
		50 freestyle
		400 IM
Main set:	5 x 100 fast on 1 minute rest	
Cool-down:	7 x 100 choice easy on 15 seconds rest	

Bike Easy 60 minute spin at HR#1

If you're tired, save it for tomorrow's long ride.

Run 30-50 minutes easy at HR#1 with drills and accelerations at end if you're not doing them on another day.

SATURDAY

Swim Optional easy 30-minute swim of your choice

Put this swim in front of the long bike today so that you get the feel for doing all three in order. This might remind you of the importance of eating early in the ride — especially after a swim!

Key Bike 240-300 minutes (4 to 5 hours) at HR#2-mid to -high

Shorter this week, but at a slightly higher intensity. The middle 1-2 hours should be steady at race pace or slightly higher.

Key Run 40-50 minute easy T-run performed at an easy to moderate effort of HR#1-2

SUNDAY

Bike Optional easy 60-90 minute ride at HR#1

If you do ride, perform your long run first.

Key Run 90-120 minutes at HR#2

Just a little harder than previous weeks, but still well in control. Keep this run aerobic.

© Fuse/Thinkstock

WEEK #22: TAPER

MONDAY

Swim Aerobic session

Warm-up:	5 x 200 as:	3 freestyle
		2 stroke *on 20 seconds rest*
Main set:	12 x 100 as:	1 drill
		2 freestyle *all easy on 15 seconds rest*
	12 x 75 as:	25 stroke
		25 freestyle
		25 stroke *on 15 seconds rest easy*
Cool-down:	400 pull easy	

TUESDAY

Key Bike Turbo

Warm-up:	15-20 min
	10 minutes steady at 90-100 RPM
	All in the aero bars at HR#3-low, with 3 minutes easy recovery spin in between.
Main set:	5 x 5 minutes steady at HR#3-mid
	two minutes in aero bars at 85-95RPM
	two minutes standing in a big gear at <80RPM
	1 minute a fast spin at above 95RPM
Cool-down:	15-20 minutes easy.

Key Run 25-35 minute transition run at HR #1-2

WEDNESDAY

Key Swim Anaerobic Threshold session		
Warm-up:	800 choice	
Main set:	8-10x 200 as:	alternate 1- 4 x 50 on 5 seconds rest
		1- 200 straight on 20 seconds rest
		all at faster than race pace or HR#3
Cool-down:	800 choice	

Bike 60 minutes easy ride at HR#1

Don't feel guilty if you take this off.

THURSDAY

Key Run Step down intervals on the track, trail, or road	
Warm-up:	15-20 minutes
	4-6 x accelerations
Main set:	4/3/2/1minutes at HR#3-low to mid
	1 minute easy in between
	3/2/1minutes at HR#3-high
	1 minute easy in between
	2/1 minutes at HR#4
	1 minute easy in between
Cool-down:	15-20 minutes easy

FRIDAY

Optional day off

Swim Sprint session

Warm-up:	300 freestyle	
	400 kick	
	500 pull	
	12 x 50 as:	25 drill
		25 kick *on 15 seconds rest*
Main set:	16 x 50 freestyle fast as:	4 on 15 seconds rest
		4 on 30 seconds rest
		4 on 45 seconds rest
		4 on 1 minute rest
Cool-down:	400 choice	

Bike 60 minute easy ride at HR#1

Run 20-40 minutes at HR#1 with drills and accelerations at end.

As with the bike ride on this day, only do it if you can do it easy and feel recovered afterwards.

SATURDAY

Swim Optional easy 30-minute swim of your choice

Key Bike 210-270 minutes at HR#2-3

This is a shorter long ride, but it is still one of your key workouts, so make sure Friday is easy or off so you are rested for the weekend workouts. Do the middle 1-2 hours at slightly faster than race pace/effort — that's IRONMAN race pace/effort!

Key Run 20-30 minute T-run at HR#2

SUNDAY

Bike Optional 60-minute easy ride at HR#1

Can't truly go easy? Don't go at all.

Key Run Only 80-90 minutes but at steady at HR#2.

Don't turn it into a race. Remember what you are training for. This should be a little faster than the other long runs, but still in control.

© iStockphoto/Thinkstock

WEEK #23: BUILD

Less is better this taper week. Let all the hard work sink in. Remember: When in doubt, go shorter, easier, or not at all!

MONDAY

Swim Aerobic session		
Warm-up:	4 x	
	2 x 100 freestyle on 10 seconds rest	
	4 x 25 choice on 5 seconds rest	
	12 x 50 as:	25 freestyle drill
		25 freestyle *on 10 seconds rest*
Main set:	4 x 200 freestyle on 20 seconds rest	
	6 x 100 freestyle on 10 seconds rest	
	4 x 25 fast on 1 minute rest	
Cool-down:	6 x 50 choice on 15 seconds rest	

TUESDAY

Key Bike Turbo	
Warm-up:	15 minutes easy,
	4 x 30 seconds fast spin
	30 seconds easy
Main set:	10/8/6/4/2 minutes steady
	at HR#3-low to -mid
	3 minutes recovery between each
	Stay in the aero position with cadence at 85-95RPM. Descending throughout is fine, but there's no need to max out on the 4 and 2 minutes intervals. If you're feeling overly wasted, just do an easy spin to help recover. Not to worry, you won't lose your fitness!
Cool-down:	15 minutes easy
Run 15-20 minute T-run at HR#1-2	

WEDNESDAY

Key Swim Anaerobic session

Warm-up:	800 choice
Main set:	3 x 800-1000 (yup, that's right. Don't panic!)
	All at HR#2 to #3-low (or at race pace/effort) on 45 seconds rest
Cool-down:	800 choice

Bike Optional 60-90 minute easy ride at HR#1

How are your feeling? If you're extremely tired, skip this ride. Still doing well and want to boost your cycling volume? Do it.

THURSDAY

Key Run Intervals

Try to do these on a trail or the road.

Warm-up:	15-20 minutes easy and stretch
Main set:	3-4 x 3 minutes pickups at HR#2-3
	with 3-5 minutes recovery between
	If you're feeling trashed, try the first 3 minute interval; if you're not feeling better just do an easy run.
Cool-down:	15-10 minutes easy

FRIDAY

Off!

SATURDAY

Swim Optional easy 30-minute swim of your choice

Remember to try to stack up at least one weekend day where you swim, ride long, then perform a T-run.

Key Bike Short and steady at HR#2-mid to –high for 120-150 minutes

Savor the taper. Try to ride at race pace that's realistic for an Ironman 112-mile bike leg.

Key Run Very short T-run of 10-15 minutes

Just to stretch out the legs after the ride. No need to sprint! Nice and controlled at HR#1-2.

SUNDAY

Bike Optional 60-minute easy ride at HR#1

If you can't do this ride easy, or you're still feeling a little trashed, then skip it.

Key Run 50-60 minutes at HR#2, nice and steady

Don't blow out the tubes: Save it for race day.

WEEK #24: RACE WEEK

MONDAY

Swim Steady swim

If possible try to get into the open water and swim a steady 40-50 minutes at what you think you could handle on race day. If stuck in the pool, then warm up for 500 meters and swim 2 x 1000 at race pace with 1 minute rest between each. 500 meter cool-down.

TUESDAY

Key Bike Easy to moderate 60-90 minute ride

Try to ride parts of the bike or run course throughout the week.

Key Run Easy to moderate 30-40 minute run

Err on the easy side.

WEDNESDAY

Key Swim Easy 30-40 minute swim, best if performed in the open water.

Work on getting used to your wetsuit if you're using one.

Run Easy 20-30 minute run. *Optional.*

THURSDAY

Swim Easy open water 20-30 minute swim

Key Bike 45-60 minute easy ride

Make sure the bike is race ready.

Key Run Short easy 20 minutes jog

FRIDAY

Optional day off

Swim Day off or easy 15 minutes to loosen you up

If any day is a good one to take off, two days before race day is it.

Bike Day off or easy 30 minutes spin

SATURDAY

Key Swim Short 5-10 minute swim mainly to wake you up and calm your nerves

Key Bike Easy 20 minutes spin

Last chance to check your race setup.

Key Run 10 minutes easy

SUNDAY

Race day! 2.4 mile swim, 112 mile bike, 26.2 mile run

QUESTIONS & ANSWERS

Q: How do I decide whether or not I should do the optional workouts?

A: It depends on how your body's recovering from the training. How are your resting heart rate, sleep quality, stress levels, muscle soreness and general mood? If you're starting to get run-down on a consistent basis (more than 3-5 days in a row), you really need to back off more during the recovery weeks. You may need to do even less than what we've recommended. Remember to keep the focus on recovering and absorbing all of the work you've done during these recovery weeks.

Q: My Ironman event falls on a Saturday, not a Sunday. How should I adjust the schedule?

A: Chop the last Wednesday plan from the schedule, and back up the last Friday workouts to Thursday. If you take a day off, you want it to be two days away from the race.

Q: I rely on knee extensions in the gym to keep my legs in order. Can I still use weights in the last couple of weeks to keep it together?

A: If you have a specific condition for which weight training keeps you healthier, by all means do what's necessary to maintain your joint's health. For most, however, the time has come to focus on sport-specific training. Your swim, bike, and run should be beginning to feel much better with the fatigue of strength training no longer in the picture.

Q. I've seen how hard it is to qualify for the Hawaii Ironman World Championship. Honestly, I'd lay my body across bullet train tracks to get a slot. What kind of advice do you have for someone whose dream it is to make it to Kona?

A. Unfortunately, there is no scientific formula for qualifying for the Hawaii Ironman. There's a certain reality to qualifying that has little to do with split times among the disciplines. You can't go off a race's history — trying to match the previous year's standard — as the temperature may hop up 15 degrees or a tornado might hit. You never know.

Our best advice for those dreaming of Hawaii is NOT to focus on qualifying itself.

Focus on having the best race you can possibly have. Don't spend it studying the other race numbers around you, trying to figure out what age-group they're in. You'll just waste energy, stress yourself out, and lose focus. Losing focus means not paying attention to your body's signals and answering them.

Don't become a triathlete seeking the Holy Grail, racing Ironmans all over the world looking for a qualifier — without enjoying a minute of it because you were so anguished about Hawaii. Your best bet is to train smart, train hard, and do your best on race day.

Q: I've never been to an Ironman and am a bit worried about what to expect during race week. I hear it can be a bit crazy. Any advice?

A: Race week at an Ironman is nuts. And yes, we do have advice — so much, in fact, it is covered in Chapter 10.

With proper preparation — and sometimes specialized equipment — even a challenged athlete can complete an Ironman.

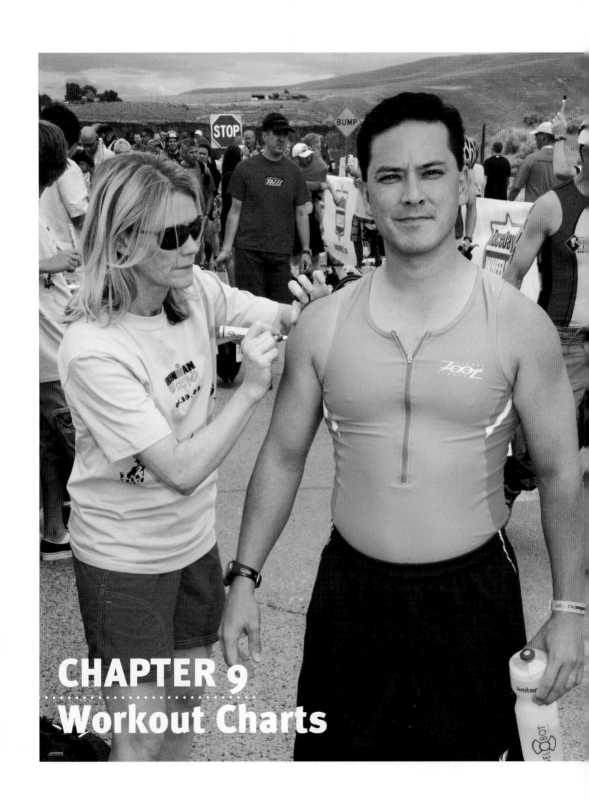

CHAPTER 9
Workout Charts

ADAPTATION PHASE

BOLD = KEY Workouts   *LIGHT* = OPTIONAL Workouts

		Swim	Bike	Run	weights
	Monday	60-90 min Technique	--	--	--
	Tuesday	--	**70 min Turbo** **Fast Spin** **3 min intervals**	**15-20 min T Run** **Easy HR#1** **off bike**	--
	Wednesday	**60-90 min** **Aerobic**	*60-90 min* *Easy HR#1-2*	--	--
Week #1	**Thursday**	60-90 min Sprint/Technique	--	**40-60 min** **Moderate**	30-60 min Adaptation 1x10 Light
	Friday	DAY OFF	DAY OFF	DAY OFF	DAY OFF
	Saturday	*30 min* *Easy Choice*	120-180 min Long Ride HR#1	**15-20 min T Run** **HR#1**	--
	Sunday	--	--	**50-70 min** **Long Run HR#1**	30-60 min Adaptation 1x10 Light

		Swim	Bike	Run	weights
	Monday	60-90 min Technique	--	--	--
	Tuesday	--	**70 min Turbo** **SLD** **5 min intervals**	**15-20 min T Run** **Easy HR#1** **off bike**	--
	Wednesday	**60-90 min** **Aerobic**	*60-90 min* *Easy HR#1-2*	--	--
Week #2	**Thursday**	60-90 min Sprint/Technique	--	**40-60 min** **Moderate**	30-60 min Adaptation 1x12 Light
	Friday	DAY OFF	DAY OFF	DAY OFF	DAY OFF
	Saturday	*30 min* *Easy Choice*	**120-180 min** **Long Ride HR#1**	15-20 min T Run HR#1	--
	Sunday	--	*60 min* *Easy HR#1*	**60-80 min** **Long Run HR#1**	30-60 min Adaptation 1x12 Light

Recovery

	Swim	Bike	Run	weights	
Monday	60-90 min Technique	--	--	--	
Tuesday	--	**70 min Turbo** **Fast Spin** **4 min intervals**	15-20 min T Run Easy HR#1 off bike	--	
Wednesday	**60-90 min** **Aerobic**	--	--	--	
Thursday	--	--	40-60 min Moderate	30-60 min Adaptation 1x15 Light	**Week #3**
Friday	DAY OFF	DAY OFF	DAY OFF	DAY OFF	
Saturday	*30 min* *Easy Choice*	**90-120 min** **Long Ride HR#1**	--	--	
Sunday	--	--	**50-70 min** **Long Run HR#1**	30-60 min Adaptation 1x15 Light	

	Swim	Bike	Run	weights	
Monday	60-90 min Technique	--	--	--	
Tuesday	--	**70 min Turbo** **Fast Spin** **6 min intervals** OR Bike AT TEST	15-20 min T Run Easy HR#1 off bike	--	
Wednesday	**60-90 min** **testing**	*60-90 min ride* *Easy HR#1*			
Thursday	--	--	70 min Track 8/7/6/5 Sub AT	30-60 min Adaptation 2x12 Light	**Week #4**
Friday *Optional OFF*	*60-90 min* *Sprint/Technique*	*60 min* *Easy Spin HR#1*	*30-50 min HR#1* *Drills & Accels at end*	--	
Saturday	30 min Easy Choice	**120-180 min** **Long Ride HR#1**	**20 min T Run** **HR#1-2**	--	
Sunday	--	*60 min* *Easy HR#1*	**70-90 min** **Long Run HR#1-2**	30-60 min Adaptation 2x15 Light	

Week #5

	Swim	Bike	Run	weights
Monday	60-90 min Technique	--	--	--
Tuesday	--	**70 min Turbo Pyramid Intervals HR#2-3**	**15-20 min T Run Easy HR#1-2 off bike**	--
Wednesday	**60-90 min AT**	*60-90 min ride Easy HR#1*	--	--
Thursday	-- Sprint/Technique	*AT TEST*	70 min Track 3 mile Sub AT TT	30-60 min Adaptation 2x15 Light
Friday *Optional OFF*	*60-90 min Sprint/Technique*	*60 min Easy Spin HR#1*	*30-50 min HR#1 Drills & Accels at end*	--
Saturday	30 min Easy Choice	**150-210 min Long Ride HR#1**	**20 min T Run HR#2**	--
Sunday	--	*60 min Easy HR#1*	**80-100 min Long Run HR#1-2**	30-60 min Adaptation 2x15 Light

Week #6

Recovery

	Swim	Bike	Run	weights
Monday	60-90 min Technique	--	--	--
Tuesday	--	**70 min Turbo Rollercoaster 5 min intervals**	**15-20 min T Run Easy HR#1 off bike**	--
Wednesday	**60-90 min Aerobic**	60-90 min ride Easy HR#1	--	--
Thursday	--	--	**40-60 min fartlek**	30-60 min Adaptation 2x15 Light
Friday	DAY OFF	DAY OFF	DAY OFF	DAY OFF
Saturday	30 min Easy Choice	**120-180 min Long Ride HR#1**	**15-20 min T Run HR#1**	--
Sunday	--	*60 min Easy HR#1*	**60-80 min Long Run HR#1-2**	30-60 min Adaptation 2x15 Light

AEROBIC BASE

	Swim	Bike	Run	weights	
Monday	60-90 min Aerobic/Technique	--	--	--	
Tuesday	--	70 min Turbo Big Gear Intervals	20-30 min T Run Easy HR#1-2 off bike	--	
Wednesday	60-90 min AT	60-90 min Easy HR#1-2	--	--	
Thursday	--	--	60-80 min Fartlek	30-60 min Endurance 2x15 Light-Medium	**Week #7**
Friday Optional OFF	60-90 min Sprint	60 min Easy HR#1	30-50 min Easy HR#1 Drills & Strides at end	--	
Saturday	30 min Easy Choice	180-240 min Long Ride HR#1-2	15-20 min T Run HR#1-2	--	
Sunday	--	60-90 min Easy HR#1	80-100 min Long Run HR#1-2	30-60 min Endurance 2x15 Light-Medium	

	Swim	Bike	Run	weights	
Monday	60-90 min Aerobic/Technique	--	--	--	
Tuesday	--	70 min Turbo Big Gear Intervals	20-30 min T Run Easy HR#1-2 off bike	--	
Wednesday	60-90 min AT	60-90 min Easy HR#1-2	--	--	
Thursday	--	--	60-80 min sub AT intervals	30-60 min Endurance 2x15 Light-Medium	**Week #8**
Friday Optional OFF	60-90 min Sprint	60 min Easy HR#1	30-50 min Easy HR#1	--	
Saturday	30-45 min Easy Choice	210-270 min Long Ride HR#1-2	15-20 min T Run HR#1-2	--	
Sunday	--	60-90 min Easy HR#1	90-105 min Long Run HR#1-2	30-60 min Endurance 2x15 Light-Medium	

Week #9

	Swim	Bike	Run	weights
Monday	60-90 min Aerobic/Technique	--	--	--
Tuesday	--	70 min Turbo Big Gear Intervals	15-20 min T Run Easy HR#1 off bike	--
Wednesday	60-90 min Aerobic/technique	60 min Easy HR#1	--	--
Thursday	--	--	40-60 min Fartlek	30-60 min Endurance 2x15 Light-Medium
Friday	DAY OFF	DAY OFF	DAY OFF	DAY OFF
Saturday	30 min Easy Choice	120-180 min Long Ride HR#1	15-20 min T Run HR#1-2	--
Sunday	--	60 min Easy HR#1	60-80 min Long Run HR#1-2	30-60 min Endurance 2x15 Light-Medium

Week #10

	Swim	Bike	Run	weights
Monday	60-90 min Aerobic/Technique	--	--	--
Tuesday	--	70 min Turbo Fast Spin	20-30 min T Run Easy HR#1-2 off bike	--
Wednesday	60-90 min at	60-90 min Easy HR#1	--	--
Thursday	--	--	60-80 min 1000m Intervals	30-60 min Endurance 2x12 Medium-Heavy
Friday Optional OFF	60-90 min Sprint	60 min Easy HR#1	30-50 min HR#1 Drills & Strides at end	--
Saturday	30 min Easy Choice	210-270 min Long Ride HR#1-2	20-30 min T Run HR#1-2	--
Sunday	--	60-90 min Easy HR#1	90-105 min Long Run HR#1-2	30-60 min Endurance 2x15 Medium-Heavy

	Swim	Bike	Run	weights	
Monday	60-90 min Aerobic/Technique	--	--	--	
Tuesday	--	**70 min Turbo** **Big Gear Intervals**	**20-30 min T Run** **HR#1-2** **off bike**	--	
Wednesday	60-90 min **AT**	60-90 min Easy HR#1	--	--	
Thursday	--	--	**60-80 min** **2-3 mile Sub AT Test**	30-60 min Endurance 2x15 Medium-Heavy	**Week #11**
Friday *Optional OFF*	*60-90 min Sprint*	*60 min Easy HR#1*	*30-50 min Easy HR#1* *Drills & Strides at end*	--	
Saturday	*30-45 min Easy Choice*	**240-300 min** **Long Ride HR#1-2**	**20-30 min T Run** **HR#1-2**	--	
Sunday	--	60-90 min Easy HR#1	**100-120 min** **Long Run HR#1-2**	30-60 min Endurance 2x15 Medium-Heavy	

Recovery

	Swim	Bike	Run	weights	
Monday	60-90 min Aerobic/Technique	--	--	--	
Tuesday	--	**70 min Turbo** **Roller coaster** **5 min intervals**	**15-20 min T Run** **HR#1** **off bike**	--	
Wednesday	60-90 min **Aerobic/Technique**	60-90 min ride Easy HR#1	--	--	
Thursday	--	--	**40-60 min** **1 min fartlek**	30-60 min Endurance 2x15 Medium-Heavy	**Week #12**
Friday	DAY OFF	DAY OFF	DAY OFF	DAY OFF	
Saturday	30 miny Easy Choice	**120-180 min** **Long Ride HR#1**	**15-20 min T Run** **HR#1**	--	
Sunday	--	*60 min Easy HR#1*	**60-80 min** **Long Run HR#1-2**	30-60 min Endurance 2x15 Medium-Heavy	

IRONMAN SPECIFIC BASE

	Swim	Bike	Run	weights
Monday	60-90 min Aerobic/Recovery	--	--	--
Tuesday	--	**75 min Turbo AT Intervals**	**25-35 min T Run HR#1-2 off bike**	--
Wednesday	**60-90 min AT**	60-90 min Easy HR#1-2	--	--
Thursday	--	--	**70-90 min 5 min intervals**	30-60 min Power or Endurance
Friday *Optional OFF*	*60-90 min Sprint*	*60 min Easy HR#1*	*30-50 min Easy HR#1 Drills & Strides at end*	--
Saturday	*30-45 min Easy Choice*	**180-240 min Long Ride HR#1-2**	**30-40 min T Run HR#1-2**	--
Sunday	--	*60-90 min Easy HR#1*	100-120 min Long Run HR#1-2	30-60 min Power or Endurance

Week #13

	Swim	Bike	Run	weights
Monday	60-90 min Aerobic/Recovery	--	--	--
Tuesday	--	**75 min Turbo 10/8/6/4 min AT Intervals**	**25-35 min T Run Easy HR#2-3 off bike**	--
Wednesday	**60-90 min AT**	60-90 min Easy HR#1-2	--	--
Thursday	--	--	**70-90 min 5 min intervals**	30-60 min Power or Endurance
Friday *Optional OFF*	*60-90 min Sprint*	*60 min Easy HR#1*	*30-50 min Easy HR#1 Drills & Strides at end*	--
Saturday	*30-45 min Easy Choice*	**240-300 min Long Ride HR#2**	**35-45 min T Run HR#1-2**	--
Sunday	--	*60-90 min Easy HR#1*	90-105 min Long Run HR#1-2	30-60 min Power or Endurance

Week #14

Recovery

	Swim	Bike	Run	weights	
Monday	60-90 min Aerobic/Recovery	--	--	--	
Tuesday	--	75 min Turbo 2 min Declining Int	15-20 min T Run Easy HR#1 off bike	--	
Wednesday	60-90 min Aerobic/technique	60 min Easy HR#1	--	--	
Thursday	--	--	40-60 min Fartlek	30-60 min Power or Endurance	**Week #15**
Friday	DAY OFF	DAY OFF	DAY OFF	DAY OFF	
Saturday	*30 min Easy Choice*	**120-180 min Long Ride HR#1**	**15-20 min T Run HR#1-2**	--	
Sunday	--	*60 min Easy HR#1*	**60-80 min Long Run HR#1-2**	30-60 min Power or Endurance	

	Swim	Bike	Run	weights	
Monday	60-90 min Aerobic/Recovery	--	--	--	
Tuesday	--	75 min Turbo AT Intervals	30-40 min T Run Easy HR#1-2 off bike	--	
Wednesday	60-90 min at	*60-90 min Easy HR#1*	--	--	
Thursday	--	--	70-90 min steady state 30 min	30-60 min Power or Endurance	**Week #16**
Friday *Optional OFF*	*60-90 min Sprint*	*60 min Easy HR#1*	*30-50 min HR#1 Drills & Strides at end*	--	
Saturday	*30-45 min Easy Choice*	**270-330 min Long Ride HR#1-2**	**40-50 min T Run HR#1-2**	--	
Sunday	--	*60-90 min Easy HR#1*	**105-120 min Long Run HR#1-2**	30-60 min Power or Endurance	

	Swim	Bike	Run	weights
Monday	60-90 min Aerobic/Recovery	--	--	--
Tuesday	--	**75 min Turbo** **12/10/8 AT Intervals**	**30-40 min T Run** **HR#1-2** **off bike**	--
Wednesday	**60-90 min** **AT**	60-90 min Easy HR#1	--	--
Thursday	--	--	**70-90 min** **longer Sub AT int**	30-60 min Chisel 2x10-12 Light-Medium
Friday *Optional OFF*	*60-90 min* *Sprint*	*60 min* *Easy HR#1*	*30-50 min Easy HR#1* *Drills & Strides at end*	--
Saturday	*30-45 min* *Easy Choice*	**330-390 min** **Long Ride HR#1-2**	**50-60 min T Run** **HR#1-2**	--
Sunday	--	*60-90 min* *Easy HR#1*	**120-150 min** **Long Run HR#1-2**	30-60 min Chisel 2x10-12 Light-Medium

Week #17

	Swim	Bike	Run	weights
Monday	60-90 min Aerobic/Recovery	--	--	--
Tuesday	--	**75 min Turbo** **AT Intervals**	**30-40 min T Run** **HR#1-2** **off bike**	--
Wednesday	**60-90 min** **AT**	60-90 min ride Easy HR#1	--	--
Thursday	--	--	**70-90 min** **steady state 40 min**	30-60 min Chisel 2x10-12 Light-Medium
Friday *Optional OFF*	*60-90 min* *Sprint*	*60 min* *Easy HR #1*	*30-50 min Easy HR#1* *Drills & Strides at end*	
Saturday	*30-45 min* *Easy Choice*	**300-360 min** **Long Ride HR#1**	**30-40 min T Run** **HR#1-2**	--
Sunday	--	*45-60 min* *Easy HR#1*	**150-180 min** **Long Run HR#1-2**	30-60 min Chisel 2x10-12 Light-Medium

Week #18

RACE PHASE

Recovery

	Swim	Bike	Run	weights	
Monday	60-90 min Aerobic/Recovery	--	--	--	
Tuesday	--	75 min Turbo 1/2/3/4/5/4/3/2/1 min intervals	15-20 min T Run HR#1 off bike	--	
Wednesday	**60-90 min Aerobic/technique**	60-90 min Easy HR#1	--	--	
Thursday	--	--	**40-60 min fartlek**	30-60 min Chisel 2x10-12 Light-Medium	**Week #19**
Friday	DAY OFF	DAY OFF	DAY OFF	DAY OFF	
Saturday	*30 min Easy Choice*	**120-180 min Long Ride HR#1-2**	**15-20 min T Run HR#1-2**	--	
Sunday *Race Day?*	--	*60-90 min Easy HR#1*	**60-80 min Long Run HR#1-2**	30-60 min Chisel 2x10-12 Light-Medium	

	Swim	Bike	Run	weights	
Monday	60-90 min Aerobic/Recovery	--	--	--	
Tuesday	--	75 min Turbo 4/8/12/8/4 min min intervals	30-40 min T Run Easy HR#2 off bike	--	
Wednesday	**60-90 min AT**	60-90 min Easy HR#1-2	--	--	
Thursday	--	--	**70-90 min 4 min intervals**	30-60 min Chisel 2x10-12 Light-Medium	**Week #20**
Friday *Optional OFF*	60-90 min Sprint	*60 min Easy HR#1*	*30-50 min Easy HR#1 Drills & Strides at end*	--	
Saturday	*30-45 min Easy Choice*	**360-420 min Long Ride HR#1-2**	**40-50 min T Run HR#1-2**	--	
Sunday	--	*60-90 min Easy HR#1*	**105-135 min Long Run HR#1-2**	30-60 min Chisel 2x10-12 Light-Medium	

		Swim	Bike	Run	weights
	Monday	60-90 min Aerobic/Recovery	--	--	--
	Tuesday	--	75 min Turbo 15/12/10 min Declining Intervals	30-40 min T Run Easy HR#2 off bike	--
	Wednesday	60-90 min Aerobic/technique	60 min Easy HR#1-2	--	--
Week #21	**Thursday**	--	--	70-90 min 2x3 mile repeats	--
	Friday	*60-90 min Sprint*	*60 min Easy HR#1*	*30-50 min Easy HR#1 Drills & Strides at end*	--
	Saturday	*30-45 min Easy Choice*	**240-300 min Long Ride HR#2**	**40-50 min T Run HR#1-2**	--
	Sunday	--	*60-90 min Easy HR#1*	**90-120 min Long Run HR#1-2**	--

TAPER

		Swim	Bike	Run	weights
	Monday	60-90 min Aerobic/Recovery	--	--	--
	Tuesday	--	75 min Turbo 10 & 15 min intervals	25-35 min T Run Easy HR#1-2 off bike	--
	Wednesday	60-90 min at	60 min Easy HR#1	--	--
Week #22	**Thursday**	--	--	60-80 min 4/3/2/1 descending intervals	--
	Friday *Optional OFF*	*60-90 min Sprint*	*60 min Easy HR#1*	*20-40 min HR#1*	--
	Saturday	*30 min Easy Choice*	**210-270 min Long Ride HR#2-3**	**20-30 min T Run HR#2**	--
	Sunday	--	60-90 min Easy HR#1	**80-90 min Long Run HR#2**	--

TAPER

	Swim	Bike	Run	weights	
Monday	60-90 min Aerobic/Recovery	--	--	--	
Tuesday	--	75 min Turbo 10/8/6/4/2/1 min intervals	15-20 min T Run HR#1-2 off bike	--	
Wednesday	60-90 min	60 min Easy HR#1	--	--	
Thursday	--	--	50-70 min 6 min intervals	--	**Week #23**
Friday	DAY OFF	DAY OFF	DAY OFF	DAY OFF	
Saturday	20-30 min Easy Choice	120-150 min Long Ride HR#2	10-15 min T Run Easy	--	
Sunday	--	60 min Easy HR#1	50-60 min HR#2	--	

Race Week!

	Swim	Bike	Run	weights	
Monday	50-60 min Steady Swim	--	--	--	
Tuesday	--	60-90 min HR#1-2	30-40 min HR#1-2	--	
Wednesday Optional OFF	30-40 min Easy	--	20-30 min Easy	--	
Thursday	20-30 min Easy	45-60 min Easy HR#1	20 min Easy	--	**Week #24**
Friday Optional OFF	15 min Sprint	30 min Easy	--	--	
Saturday	5-10 min just get wet	20 min Easy	10 min Easy	--	
Sunday	RACE DAY! 2.4 miles	RACE DAY! 112 miles	RACE DAY! 26.2 miles	RACE DAY!	

CHAPTER 10
Race Week

Congratulations on making it this far! Now all you have to do is race! Here are some suggestions to help you make the best of your event.

PREPARE SO RACE WEEK IS SANE

If you've ever been to an Ironman, you know how the days preceding the race are thick with stress and how nerves are rattled. Already edgy because tapering is driving them crazy, triathletes unprepared for the myriad meetings, check-ins and deadlines start to lose it. Don't be one of them. Using material from your race information package and/or the race website, carefully plan the itinerary of what you need to get done and when you need to do it. Avoid the rush to check-ins by getting there early. Everything you need to know to do this is available to you; there's no excuse for being unprepared. Don't let it freak you out.

TRAVEL WISELY

Whether you're driving or flying, be rested before you go. Too many athletes arrive at their race with some kind of cold that they didn't have when they left home. When you are in hard training, your immune defenses can become depressed. Get rested and don't make the mistake of having an epic training day on the day (or the day before) you get on a plane. By the same token, the first workout you do the day after you arrive should be at a lower than normal intensity!!

Stay hydrated while you are traveling.

GET A NEW PAIR OF GOGGLES

You can purchase a new pair of goggles for as little as $10. I know that this is an expensive sport – but, if you have made the investment necessary to get to the line, don't show up on race morning with a foggy, scratched pair of goggles. Make the big buy — get a pair that fits and you can see out of. It is always a good idea to have an extra pair in your swim bag in case the strap decides to break on race morning. For many triathletes, it is a wonderful surprise to have goggles that are comfortable and clear when they have been swimming in the haze of their "old favorites" for the past year and a half.

PUT ON YOUR SUNSCREEN FIRST

Put on your sunscreen BEFORE you put on your race outfit!!! Don't put on your swimsuit and put sunscreen on around it. Your suit will hike up on the bike and you will burn those parts that have never seen the sun.

WEAR A HAT DURING THE RUN

We suggest wearing a hat (not a visor) during the run. The lighter the color, the better. Choose something that fits comfortably and has room to put ice in as you're racing. If it's a particularly hot day, this can be a great way to keep your core temperature down between aid stations. Make sure you ask for ice as you approach the aid station and they will have it ready for you when you get there. If you plan to be running at night, it still might be a good idea.

As with all of these suggestions, do what you know will work, not what sounds like a good idea. Try anything new in your training — not on race day.

PACE YOURSELF

It should be obvious that pacing in an Ironman distance event is crucial to a successful day — but we'll repeat ourselves. Pace yourself in each discipline. Be realistic and don't (DO NOT) go anaerobic. It's too costly and you will end up paying later.

Those who intend to be competitive within your division may touch the anaerobic level a time or two (start of the swim, hills on the bike, etc.), but it's important to know what you can handle. If this is your first Ironman and/or you simply want to have your best possible finish and not test limits (aren't the phrases "not testing limits" and "doing an Ironman" oxymoronic? Yes, but . . .), stay on the aerobic side of intensity!

Paying attention to the details will help smooth your flight to the finish line.

DURING THE RACE, STAY CALM AND FOCUSED

Ironman is a long event. There will be a lot of high and low points. You may get called for drafting. You may get a flat tire. You may miss a bottle exchange on the bike. You may have to wait 30 seconds for the volunteers to find your special needs bag. You may get smacked in the head in the swim. You may lose your goggles in the swim. You may be reduced to walking at the start of the run. Almost anything can (and will) happen.

Above all, stay focused on your primary goal: to have fun and finish the race. We have seen too many athletes blow their races unnecessarily because they didn't keep their poise and adapt to the current situation. Get a flat? Fix it. (By the way, always carry at least one spare and a pump and/or several "quick-fills" on the bike.) Get a drafting call? Listen to the marshal, do what they tell you to do and take advantage of the bonus recovery time (in fact, have a plan for how best to use such time. Stretching, for example). Getting whacked in the swim? Simply swim away from the situation. Don't waste time and energy fighting it.

Paula Newby-Fraser keeps in her mind: "You can always slow down!" Doesn't sound like it would come out of her racing brain, but remembering this simple sentence will keep you out of trouble in many situations. When you hit a low point and feel like you can't go on, simply do what you would do in training: slow down. Stay present and ask yourself: "What do I need right now?" Look at all of your options and take corrective action.

RUN THE TANGENTS

The shortest distance between two points is a straight line, and it would be nice to make the marathon as short as possible (right?). Unless you're told otherwise (make sure you're at the pre-race meeting or that you bring this up with an official before the event). There is usually no rule about crossing the center line of the road on the run (is there?). While you must keep your head up for upcoming aid-stations — and, more importantly, to avoid oncoming runners and cyclists — you can shave off significant distance by running the shortest line along the course. While you need to listen to what race officials tell you, don't be a sheep and mindlessly follow those in front of you. At the very least you can run the tangents of whichever side of the road you're on.
Always be aware of what is going on around you and how you can get to the finish line as efficiently and quickly as possible.
Expect nothing and be ready for anything!

QUESTIONS & ANSWERS

Q. I've become fairly adept at transitions for shorter triathlons. Do you have any pointers for Ironman transitions?

A. Yes, especially for first-timers in the Ironman. Like bike position, it's about comfort. Take your time — it's a very long day, and if you screw up with your clothing in transition, it's going to be a very long and very uncomfortable day. So don't rush! Get fully and comfortably changed before you head out on the bike or on the run.

If you're in a more competitive mode and time is money, think through your clothing and find ways to trim your transition to-do list. For example, find shorts you can ride and run in. Sew your race number to your top and make a pocket out of it for gels and energy bars. If it's a wetsuit-legal Ironman, remember that you can wear your bike apparel under the suit. Master your transition — it should be second nature by race day. Never, never rush!!!

Q. What's your thinking on special needs bags?

A. We feel the special needs bags should be used for the following purposes:
1. Back up. Put necessities you have to have (e.g., salt tabs, anti-acids, photo of dog) in your special needs bags, items that you may have accidentally dropped or lost while racing.
2. Items you can't get from aid stations. Think of the food or drink that you remember eating five hours into a long ride as "the BEST thing I've ever tasted." In other words, if a Snickers bar saved your butt on your last long ride, pop it into the special needs bag. That's the kind of thing we're talking about. Whatever you do, don't put crap in there that IS available at every aid station. If bananas are served on the course, which is almost always the case, the last thing you're going to want is an extra banana.
3. Clothing. If you're going to be out there until after the sun goes down, use the marathon special needs bag for something to help keep you warm.

Q. Should I wear a heart rate monitor during the race?

A. The decision to wear (or not wear) a heart rate monitor (HRM) in a race is an extremely individual and personal choice. The primary reasons to do so are:
1. Direct information. To keep race intensities at a realistic and optimal level so

that you can sustain the highest average speed throughout the race... WITHOUT blowing up.

2. Post race/future planning. To provide post race information that can be analyzed for the purpose of adjusting: nutrition and hydration strategies; pacing strategies; determining the best way to approach differing geographical features of a course; determining the best way to approach differing weather conditions, etc. All of this would be based on heart rate information related to the performance on the day.

When you consider the fact that 99% of the world, national, and even personal records for endurance athletes are achieved with an "even pacing" strategy (the pace is the same from the start of an event to the finish) OR a "negative splitting" strategy (the pace of the second half of the event is faster than the first half), the value of using an HRM becomes apparent.

You've probably witnessed (or experienced) inappropriate pacing strategies if you've ever done a 5km or 10km running race. People go out in the first quarter to third of the race at paces that are anywhere from 30 seconds to two minutes per mile faster than their finishing average pace. For example: Joe Runner just ran a 22 minute 5k. This equates to a 7:06 per mile pace. It's interesting to note that Joe went out in a first mile of 5:45, second mile of 7:00, third mile of 7:50, and brought home the final .1 miles (~200 meters) in 1:25. This is how NOT to pace yourself.

The difficulty in determining appropriate pace is even more exaggerated in longer distance events because the levels of perceived effort become much more subtle. Race pace for an Ironman is much lower than race pace for an Olympic distance or sprint triathlon, but both feel pretty much the same in the early stages. The potential to go out too hard in a longer event is much greater and exacerbated by lack of experience.

This is where using an HRM in a race can save you from more pain and suffering than is necessary. By adhering to heart rate zones that you know (through training), you'll be able to maintain for the given distance, and you maximize your chances of finishing as close to your current potential as possible.

Yet, we must also stress the importance of emotion and intuition. Remember Greg Lemond's victory at the ,89 Tour de France? He faced what was considered an impossible situation on the final day of the Tour that year. The last stage was a 16-mile time trial. He was some 50 seconds behind Laurent Fignon in the standings and, it was thought, if Fignon rode even a mediocre time trial, he'd win for sure. Lemond told his team director and team car that he wanted NO information regarding times or splits and he did NOT wear an HRM to monitor his performance. He raced on pure emotion and a singular focus on going hard. As you know, he ended up doing that time trial just fast enough to win what was the closest finish in the Tour de France history. Granted, Lemond was racing a relatively short event where pacing was less of an issue, but it demonstrated the fact that, sometimes, keeping track of objective information like time and heart rate can put a limit (even if it's psychological) on your performance.

All of that said, there are huge benefits to be gained from wearing an HRM in events that are longer than 1.5-2 hours, when pacing becomes more critical. Especially if you have limited training and racing self-knowledge, an HRM can be a savior that allows a much more positive event experience. It can take the guesswork out of the puzzle when trying to determine whether or not the pace is too slow or fast. It also is a good tool to teach the crucial relationship among pace, heart rate and perceived effort.

PRE-RACE CHECKLIST

SWIM
- Swim suit
- Wet suit (if applicable)
- Goggles (extra pair?)
- Swim cap (race provided)
- Petroleum jelly (or Body Glide or Sportslick)
- Towel (to lay on ground in transition & for post race)
- Sunscreen

BIKE
- Bike (duh)
- Bike shoes
- Helmet
- Sunglasses
- Bike outfit (shorts & jersey, etc.)
- Pump
- Water bottles
- Spare tire / tube
- CO2 cartridges and/or frame pump
- Sunscreen

RUN
- Running shoes
- Run clothing (if different from swim & bike)
- Hat
- Sunglasses
- Sunscreen

WHAT ELSE?
- Post race drink / food
- Post race clothing
- Duct tape
- Zip ties
- Bike tools
- Floor pump with accurate gauge
- First aid kit
- Magic Marker (to mark your race # with)
- Toilet paper
- Etc.

Organizing your race needs ahead of time can help you get out of the transition areas faster. We recommend practicing transitions as well as doing a tune-up race to work the kinks out.

CHAPTER 11
Ironman Nutrition

The night before the 1992 Hawaiian Ironman, Paula Newby-Fraser's dinner consisted of 4-5 slices of Domino's bacon-cheeseburger pizza, about three leaves of lettuce and a quarter to a third of a pan of brownies (slightly undercooked and still warm). We don't remember what she drank, but we do but recall her putting milk on her brownies. The next day, she set the course record for women of 8:55.

There you go. There's the magic formula you've been waiting for.

Before anything is else said regarding this topic, we must give a resounding disclaimer. We're not registered dieticians or doctors; we have no graduate degrees in nutrition. Between us, we have had the opportunity to observe and experience the eating habits of some of the best professional triathletes at first hand, and we have been known to "put it away" ourselves every now and then ("Wow, they must be real experts!").

Nutrition is something that has intrigued many people for years. What, after all, could be more relevant to health and well being, not to mention athletic performance, than what we put into our bodies day after day for a lifetime (how ‚bout lifestyle, environment, genetics and mental/spiritual health)? Being human and, therefore, always looking for "the answer," we seem to grab onto the conclusions of the latest study as though this will finally be the cure for whatever ails us.

Some of the best advice we've heard was given to Huddle on his first day of Nutrition 101 at the University of Arizona. The professor wrote three words on the overhead: Variety and Moderation.

Simple.

Perhaps it was too simple. To think that getting by optimally merely required the moderate consumption of a wide variety of foods seems too … simple.

The most relevant questions to tackle in this book are pre-race, during the race, and post-race nutrition. To give you a specific dietary plan would, in our opinion, be a bit presumptuous and very prejudiced to our own dietary idiosyncrasies. Why don't we let you decide for yourself what guidelines (regular or non-fat Twinkies) you want to follow and give you our two cents on what we consider to be important to the Ironman.

KEY POINTS FOR PRE-RACE NUTRITION:

- Different individuals will thrive on both liquid and solid forms of pre-race foods. Experiment in training with both forms before your event.

- Eat your pre-race breakfast between two to four hours before the start. Try to take in about 500-800 calories of liquid and solid calories. Experiment for this using your weekend long training sessions.

- Weather conditions (heat/humidity vs. cold/dry) will play a huge role in what form of and how many calories can be consumed and/or kept down (absorbed). Once again, experiment before race day, in similar conditions if possible and, if not, during events of less importance.

- Spread out your pre-race meal. Consume most of the calories early on, but allow yourself to spread the meal over 1-2 hours. For example, go from your English muffin and yogurt first thing, to sipping fluid replacement drinks (Gatorade, Race-Day, etc.) in the final half hour to hour prior to your start time.

RACE NUTRITION

The factors you need to consider with regard to nutrition during a race are:

- Your caloric needs
- The distance/intensity of the race
- The conditions you expect to face (hot, cool, humid, etc.)
- What will be available at the event's aid stations

So, what surprises will you be in for during an Ironman compared to an Olympic distance event? It's longer (DUH!!!) and performed at a lower intensity than an Olympic distance event. Hydration, sodium intake and consuming calories in an Ironman are major concerns.

How do you determine your caloric needs and can you eat too much during a race? Remember that, regardless of all the scientific knowledge on how much an athlete burns during a given activity, you are limited not by how much you burn but by how much your body can ABSORB. Studies have shown that, during aerobic activity, the maximum number of calories a 150 lb. male can absorb is in the neighborhood of 250-275 per hour. While there are athletes who believe you can train yourself to be able to absorb more (Mark Allen felt he could handle 400-500 calories per hour), this is a good starting point. If you weigh less than 150 lbs., scale this number (250-275) back. In training, you can practice getting your calories down while going at distances and intensities that mimic race levels. This, more than any numbers on paper, will give you the feedback you need to determine how much you can or can't handle.

Keep in mind that conditions and intensity affect how many calories you will be able to get down and in what form. While we have no scientific research on the topic, it seems that heat and humidity make it more difficult to get down calories, so the source needs to be as dilute and bland as possible. By the same token, cooler conditions are usually more conducive to caloric consumption and absorption.

Practice eating when you train. It's not the most comfortable thing to do, but in an Ironman you won't have enough glycogen (the preferred fuel source for working muscles) on board to carry you to the finish line efficiently. If possible, find out what fluid replacement drink the event will be supplying — Gatorade, Powerade, RaceDay, etc. — and practice with it.

The last thing to add here is that, nutritionally speaking, what works one weekend might not work on the following weekend. Try to be consistent but, when your old favorite is no longer cutting it, don't be afraid to try something new!

KEY POINTS FOR RACE NUTRITION

Experiment in training with both liquid and solid types of food before your event. Use your long training sessions as a lab.

- Weather conditions (heat/humidity vs. cold/dry) will play a huge role in what form of and how many calories can be consumed and/or kept down (absorbed). Once again, experiment before race day, in similar conditions if possible and, if not, during events of less importance.

- In an Ironman event (and depending on how much you found you could absorb in training), you should aim for an intake of 250-300 calories per hour.

- Spread your hourly during-race fueling needs over 15 to 20 minute increments (don't try to get it all down on the hour!). Because it's typically easier to eat (and absorb) on the bike, try to take in a lot of your calories in the first three-quarters of the bike. For example, if you found that 300 calories per hour is your magic number, try to take in 100 calories every 20 minutes or, better yet, 75 calories every 15 minutes.

- If solid foods are going to be consumed, get them down early on in the bike leg, as they will likely be more palatable then than during the run.

- In your Ironman race, make sure you account for the time spent during the swim. Upon exiting the water, try to get a few extra (75-150cal) calories down quickly.

- Gels and solid foods (concentrated calories) are best absorbed when combined with water/fluid replacement drink.

POST-RACE NUTRITION

There is much that could be said about what and how much to eat after a race... but we're going to stick to the most important points.

- The first order of business after crossing the finish line should be re-hydration. Water and fluid replacement fill this need quite well.

- There is a well-established "carbohydrate window" where your muscles have the best opportunity to refuel optimally. The current recommendation is to consume 100 grams (400 calories) of carbohydrate within the first one-half to two hours immediately following an event / training session. Simple carbohydrates (e.g. fluid replacement drinks, cookies, fruit, etc.) are more easily absorbed than complex carbohydrates. Beyond two hours, the "window of opportunity" diminishes greatly, and the chance to become optimally recovered decreases as well.

- After two hours, you should eat a well-balanced meal that includes protein, fat and carbohydrate. Such a meal can be consumed as soon as you're ready to eat.

- Eat nutritiously throughout the week, with plenty of good protein, to help fuel your body's complete recovery.

HYDRATION AND HYPONATREMIA

A key part of the "nutrition" topic must include what is, many times, even more important than how many calories you get down your throat: Hydration. Though it should go without saying, your hydration status, in any given endurance event, will be a big determinant how well you perform. Studies show that losses of even two to three percent of your total body weight in fluid can result in a significant decrease in performance.

With this in mind, let's consider some basic hydration strategies. Here are some good points on the subject taken from the Gatorade Sports Science Exchange:

- Weigh in without clothes before and after exercise, especially during hot weather. For each pound of body weight lost during exercise, drink two cups of fluid.

- Drink a re-hydration beverage containing sodium to quickly replenish lost body fluids. The beverage also contains 6-8% sucrose or glucose.

- Drink two-and-one-half cups of fluid two hours before practice or competition.

- Drink one-and-one-half cups of fluid 15 minutes before the event.

- Drink at least one cup of fluid every 15-20 minutes during training and competition.

- Do not restrict fluids before or during an event.

One point we'd like to harp on a little: Don't rely solely on water for hydration. In fact, if possible rely more on fluid replacement drinks (provided they are mixed at a concentration that suits you). People have run into severe problems by taking in too much water in long, hot events (like Ironman races). You must be conscious of your electrolyte status (the key element being sodium). Depending on who you are, you will lose 1 to 3 grams (1000-3000 mg) of sodium per hour in your sweat. On a particularly hot day, this will be a big problem if the event is longer than four hours.

You can avoid potential problems associated with hyponatremia (low blood sodium levels) by using fluid replacement drinks in addition to water, by lightly salting your food in the week leading up to a long, hot event, and by not overdoing your intake of water.

Some athletes (ourselves included) have used buffered salt tablets by the brand name of ThermoTabs to prevent the problems associated with hyponatremia. Each tablet has 450 mg of sodium in it and, if the day is particularly hot, these can be a lifesaver. One to two tablets per hour taken with water or fluid replacement can be the difference between finishing comfortably or cramping and having to walk the last 10 miles. Buffered salt tablets aren't a magic bullet, but they are certainly safe and, if you know that you tend toward these kinds of problems, can be a big help. As with anything, try them in training before using them in a race. Other sources of salt include potato chips (no, we're not kidding), pretzels, etc.

We're not saying don't hydrate — but simply that you can use a fluid replacement drink to hydrate as well as water. Once you're peeing clear, you're hydrated! This is an especially relevant sentence the night before an event. If your urine is clear, quit drinking, get some sleep, and you can continue re-hydrating when you wake up in the morning.

VITAMIN & MINERAL SUPPLEMENTS

There are those who are adamant that if you eat a "normal, healthy" diet, you will have no problem getting all the nutrients necessary to maintain health and even support any extracurricular, psychotic, over-training activity. Once again, we disagree.

Okay, let's take that back. We disagree for the percentage of the population that this is aimed at — that is the type A, hard driven, endurance sport aficionado and even, perhaps to a lesser degree, for anyone (who eats a "healthy diet"?). "Cut to the chase. What vitamins should I be taking?"

We would recommend a multi-vitamin and mineral combination.

You can go completely overboard, it can get expensive and, according to some people (like your M.D.) will not do you any good. You could very well be paying for no other effect than expensive urine.

We'll tell you what we take/have taken and let you decide. Keep in mind that the brands mentioned are simply examples of a supplement or supplement combination. There are thousands of other brands which contain the same formula(s). Our daily in-season vitamin regimen** is as follows:

- 3-6 Living Source** – Master Nutrient System multi-vitamin & mineral tablets or 1 Nutriguard** Athletes Meal Pack (taken before noon with a meal). These two products cover the majority of our personal requirements for vitamins, minerals, and anti-oxidants.

- 1 Trader Joe's** vitamin E capsule (400 IU) taken before noon with meal

- 1-3 Trader Joe's 1000mg vitamin C tablets taken before noon with meal and sometimes over the course of the day

- 1 Trader Joe's anti-oxidant formula tablet

- 1 Trader Joe's B vitamin combination

*(**Brand is mentioned only for specificity.
We're not advocating one brand over another.)*

ANTI-OXIDANTS

Perhaps one of the most relevant problems with endurance athletes is that they produce abnormal levels of free radicals. This build-up has been shown to cause damage at the cellular level, leading to impairment of health and your ability to adequately recover from endurance activity.

Free radical damage can be significantly reduced with the supplementation of anti-oxidants. Anti-oxidants include:

Good nutrition — both during training and on race day — helps your body handle challenges on the course.

- Vitamin A in the form of beta-carotene
- Vitamin C
- Vitamin E
- selenium
- zinc
- bioflavonoids
- grape seed extract
- pycogenol
- alpha lipoic acid

While it's unreasonable to expect you to take all of the above — and there are many different combina-tions you could take, a common (and safe) regimen might include:

- 25,000 IU Beta-carotene
- 1000mg of vitamin C
- 400 IU vitamin E
- 300 mcg selenium.

CHAPTER 12
Resources

CYCLING

NCBW, 1612 K Street, NW, Washington DC 20006, www.bikewalk.com

International Mountain Biking Assn, nonprofit group that promotes mountain biking, PO Box 7578, Boulder, CO 80306, 303/545-9011, Imba@aol.com, www.imba.com

League of American Bicyclists, national membership organization, 1612 K Street NW, Ste. 401, Washington DC, 20006, 202/822-1333, www.bikeleague.org

United States Cycling Federation, governing body for amateur cycling, One Olympic Plaza, Colorado Springs, CO 80909-5775, 719/578-4581, www.usacycling.org

United States Professional Cycling Federation, governing body for professional cycling, One Olympic Plaza, Colorado Springs, CO 80909, 719/578-4581

RUNNING/TRACK & FIELD

American Running & Fitness Assn, not-for-profit organization to educate runners and other fitness enthusiasts, 4405 E/W Highway #405, Bethesda, MD 20814, 800-776-2732, www.arfa.org

Road Runners Club of America (RRCA), national association of running clubs, 1150 S. Washington Street #250, Alexandria, VA 22314, 703/836-0558, e-mail office@rrca.org, website www.rrca.org

USA Track & Field, national governing body for road racing, cross country, track & field & race walking events, PO Box 120, Indianapolis, IN 46206, 317/261-0500, www.usaff.org

SWIMMING

Aquatic Exercise Assn, resource center for aquatic fitness (vertical exercise in the pool), PO Box 1609, Nokomis, FL 34274, 941/486-8600, www.aeawave.com

U.S. Swimming, One Olympic Plaza, Colorado Springs, CO 80809, 719/578-4578, www.usaswimming.org

TRIATHLON

USA Triathlon Federation, 5825 Delmonico Drive, Colorado Springs, CO 80910, 719/597-9090, membership services, 800-874-1872, www.usatriathlon.org

World Triathlon Corporation, Ironman Mainland Office, PO Box 1608, Tarpon Springs, FL 34688, 813/942-4767, www.ironmanlive.com

HOT LINKS

www.active.com
Nationwide source for thousands of participatory sports events.

www.fitnesszone.com
Shop fitnesszone.com for bikes, free-weights, aerobic supplies, etc. Obtain free fitness profiles, online fitness articles, gym locator (locate any gym in the U.S.). Fitness forums, classifieds, fitness library.

www.runnersworld.com
Training tips, recent issue articles, nutrition tips, travel, statistics, shoes, awards, forums, injury prevention tips and descriptions.

www.acefitness.org
American Council on Exercise. Fit facts, news releases, find a certified professional.

www.insidetri.com
Find a triathlon.

www.multisports.com
Current news, events and archives on multi-sports.

www.triathlete-competitor.com
Current news and archives on the sport of triathlon.

www.competitor.com
Current news, events and archives on multi-sports in Southern California.

www.eatright.org/find.html
Find a nutritionist near you.

ABOUT THE AUTHORS

PAUL HUDDLE
Endurance Multi Sport Coach

During his twelve-year career as a professional triathlete, Paul Huddle finished over twenty Ironman distance events (nine in Hawaii) and well over 300 triathlons. He was top-ten finisher at the Ironman Triathlon World Championship in Kona, Hawaii in 1990, '92 and '93; with a best time of 8:27:24. He won Ironman Japan ('91); the International Strongman Triathlon ('91, '93); the Ironhorse Triathlon; and the Wildflower Triathlon (1989 & 1991). He also had top-five finishes at Ironman Lanzarote, New Zealand, Canada and Japan.

As a partner in Multisports.com, Huddle is involved in production, administration and instruction at triathlon camps and clinics all over the world. Multisports.com produces annual adult camps and offers on-line coaching for swimming, running, cycling and triathlon for athletes of all levels of ability. Huddle co-writes the popular column, "Dear Coach" for Triathlete Magazine and personally coaches Paula Newby-Fraser, Chris Legh, Spencer Smith and several age group champions at both the Ironman and Olympic distances.

With a B.S. in Food Science from the University of Arizona at Tucson, he is a member of USA Triathlon's Coaching Advisory Board for the design and implementation of athlete and coaching competency requirements and was certified as a Sport, Expert and Elite level coach by USA Cycling at the Olympic Training Center in Colorado Springs, CO. He has also been certified by the American Council on Exercise (ACE) as a Personal Trainer.

T. J. MURPHY
Triathlete/Writer/Collaborator

T. J. Murphy's first triathlon was the All Iowa Half-Ironman in 1983, where he shrewdly cut down on his time in transitions by doing the whole race in a pair of yellow Sub-4 running shorts. Since then, he not only discovered bike shorts, but managed to find the finish line in four Ironman events, including the Hawaii Ironman in 2000. Formerly the editor-in-chief of Triathlete Magazine, he is now editor of CitySports Magazine in San Francisco and a regular contributer to Ironmanlive.com.

ROCH FREY
Endurance Multi Sport Coach

A former professional triathlete from Canada, Roch Frey has been involved with triathlon for over twenty years. After winning the Canadian Long Course National Champions- hips in 1993, he turned to full-time coaching and founded the UCSD Master's Triathlon Training Club. He built a triathlon training program in San Diego's north county and works with 15-20 triathletes each year on a one-to-one basis, including Heather Fuhr, 1997 Ironman Hawaii Champion and Peter Reid, 1998 and 2000 Ironman Hawaii Champion.

In 1999, Frey combined forces with Paul Huddle, Paula Newby-Fraser and John Duke to create Multisports.com. They hold triathlon-training camps throughout the world. In addition, he and Paul Huddle established online training programs that cover all distances of triathlons from sprint to Ironman and accommodates all levels of triathletes.

In 2000, Frey took his coaching expertise to the sport of Adventure Racing. He and Huddle were the head coaches for the Asian MSOQ Team, spending several weeks in China preparing the team for this four-day stage event. With Huddle, he writes Triathlete Magazine's "Dear Coach" column, and serves as race and course director for a variety of events.

Frey has a B.S. in Physical Education, Coaching/Exercise Physiology from the University of Alberta. A graduate of the National Coaching Certification Program (NCCP) in Canada, he holds certificates in Level 3 Theory, Level 3 Technical, Triathlon Level 2 Technical, Swimming, Cycling, Running and Level 1 Paddling Instructor. He is a member of the American Swim Coaches Association, USA Triathlon and Triathlon Canada.

INDEX

PHOTO CREDITS

Cover photo: imago
Photos: Bakke-Svensson/Ironman, see individual photos
Cover design: Sabine Groten